*Data Protection in the Financial Services
Industry*

Data Protection in the Financial Services Industry

MANDY WEBSTER

Routledge
Taylor & Francis Group

LONDON AND NEW YORK

First published 2006 by Gower Publishing

Published 2016 by Routledge
2 Park Square, Milton Park, Abingdon, Oxon OX14 4RN
711 Third Avenue, New York, NY 10017, USA

Routledge is an imprint of the Taylor & Francis Group, an informa business

British Library Cataloguing in Publication Data
Webster, Mandy
  Data protection in the financial services industry
  1. Financial services industry – Great Britain – Management
  2. Financial services industry – Law and legislation – Great
  Britain 3. Data protection – Great Britain 4. Data protection
  – Law and legislation – Great Britain
  I. Title
  332'.024'0068

  ISBN 9780566086625 (hbk)

Library of Congress Cataloging-in-Publication Data
Webster, Mandy.
  Data protection in the financial services industry / by Mandy Webster.
    p. cm.
  Includes index.
  ISBN 0-566-08662-X
  1. Data protection--Law and legislation--Great Britain. 2. Financial services industry--Security measures--Great Britain. I. Title.

  KD3756.W43 2005
  342.4108'58--dc22

                                                                    2005015274

Typeset by N²productions.

Contents

PART 1

The Principles

Part I considers data protection from the legal perspective. It focuses on the Data Protection Act 1998 (the Act), which codifies much of the law relating to data protection in the UK. It starts by considering technical definitions used in the Act and moves through an in-depth consideration of the eight data protection principles. The principles are the backbone of data protection law. They are statements of good personal data management and practice.

The principles are set out in Schedule 1 to the Act. The schedule is divided into two parts. Part I contains the bare text of the principles. Part II is entitled 'Interpretation of the Principles in Part I' and sets out additional requirements for compliance with the principles as well as providing interpretation and guidance on compliance standards.

Schedule 1 is incorporated into the Act by section 4(4) of the Act. Section 4 also provides that it is the duty of a data controller to comply with the principles in relation to all personal data of which it is the data controller. There is no duty on data processors to comply with the principles. As a result, the distinction between data controllers and data processors is critical and a significant part of Chapter 11 is devoted to identifying and analysing the relationship between data controllers and data processors.

Each chapter on the principles starts with a short introduction, and goes on to consider the actual wording of the principle or subject right; this is followed by an analysis of the meaning. The interpretive provisions are also explored and any relevant guidance from the Information Commissioner on meeting the compliance standard is given and explained. Relevant examples are provided where these are appropriate.

Guidance published by the Information Commissioner that assists in understanding the legal requirements is included. As the data protection principles are largely unchanged from their introduction under the Data Protection Act 1984, reference is made to guidance issued in relation to the 1984 Act where it is thought to be still relevant and helpful in interpreting current law.

CHAPTER 1

Introduction

The financial services industry is a long-established industry in the UK. Data protection law has been in effect here since as recently as 1984.[1] Yet, interestingly, more myths surround data protection law than the financial services sector. The term 'financial services' is used to describe savings, investments, insurance, and credit. Can we be as certain of what is meant by 'data protection'? As a simple definition, data protection means the law protecting the privacy of individuals and regulating the activities of organisations that use information relating to individuals.

There has been debate about how far the law is going in introducing a right to privacy in the UK. The government has stated that it has no wish to introduce a statutory right to privacy and the courts are reluctant to create a new tort of invasion of privacy. In *Naomi Campbell* v. *Daily Mirror*,[2] the decision in Ms Campbell's favour was decided partly on the fact that the information being made public related to her health and publication of that information might be detrimental to her health in future. In *Douglas* v. *Hello!*,[3] the Court of Appeal noted that it was being put under pressure by human rights legislation and recent European cases to protect individuals from invasion of privacy and turned to breach of confidence to find in favour of the Douglases, although *OK!* magazine, the co-complainants, did not have the same right of confidence. Statutes such as the Human Rights Act 2000[4] and the Data Protection Act 1998[5] (the Act) introduce a number of individual rights which collectively start to add up to a right to privacy.

A widespread myth is that business in the UK is subject to more regulation and higher compliance standards than elsewhere. Member states of the European Union (EU) have mandated to operate as a single market. The corollary to that mandate is that many laws have been harmonised to reduce the differences between the member states and to give effect to the free flow of goods, persons, services and capital within the EU. This harmonisation includes data protection law, so not only is the law based on standards set out in the European Commission (EC) Directive,[6] its provisions are

---

1   The Data Protection Act 1984 introduced data protection law to Britain.
2   For example *Naomi Campbell* v. *MGN Ltd* [2004] UKHL22.
3   *Douglas and others* v. *Hello! Ltd and others (no. 3)* [2005] EWCA Civ 595.
4   Article 8 states that a citizen has the right to privacy of family life and correspondence.
5   See chapters 4 to 12 on the data protection principles.
6   The Data Protection Act 1998 is derived from EC Directive 95/46/EC.

largely the same as those that apply in France, Italy, Spain, Germany, the Netherlands and so on.

Another myth is that there is no need to comply with data protection law unless you are registered for data protection. Like the 1984 Act, the 1998 Act requires organisations involved in certain, specified, activities to have their details recorded on the public data protection register. However, a quirk of the 1984 Act meant that unless an organisation was registered for data protection, there was no requirement to comply with the other provisions of the Act. That anomaly has been swept away by the 1998 Act. Specifically, all organisations that use personal information must comply with the Act,[7] regardless of the need to notify (the term for 'registration' adopted from the European Commission (EC) Directive). Since all businesses utilise some personal information, for example information relating to employees, agents and directors, it follows that all businesses must comply with the Act.

The most recent myth, especially among small businesses, is that regulated businesses need only comply with the regulator's handbook (the regulator is currently the Financial Services Authority (FSA)). This is not the case; the *FSA Handbook*[8] supplements UK legislation; it does not replace it. Member firms must adhere to the provisions of all relevant UK laws.

The myths about financial services arise from the complexity of its products and services; many products have been designed to maximise tax advantages available from time to time, and this does not lend itself to simplicity. Another factor is the ever-present bundling of products to 'make it simpler for the customer' and to maximise revenue from new customers; for example, general insurance products are usually offered with legal expenses insurance, motor insurance with breakdown cover, and so on.

The bundling of products leads some organisations to specialise in key competences. Legal expenses insurance tends to be provided by one or two insurance companies and other general insurance companies outsource the administration of legal expenses cover to those companies. Broking and other intermediary organisations specialise in simply advising on products and services available from a variety of product providers. Other organisations support sales networks by providing financial and regulatory administration and monitoring. Organisations with high-profile brand names, especially outside the financial services sectors, might allow the brand name and their distribution channel to be used to promote branded financial products while outsourcing the product design and administration to financial services specialists.

---

7   Section 4(4) of the Data Protection Act 1998.
8   FSA (2005) *FSA Handbook*. Available from fsahandbook.info/FSA.

Specialisation may be driven by regulation; many financial products and services can only be supplied by appropriately authorised organisations; for example, deposit taking is restricted to banks and building societies and insurance to insurance companies authorised by the FSA. Authorisation involves compliance with minimum capital and liquidity requirements, which may act as a barrier to new entrants to the market; therefore an alternative solution is to outsource to those organisations that are already established and that already have authorisation.

There are a variety of distributors for financial products and services, which adds another level of complexity. Most product providers undertake direct sales as well as sales via intermediaries. The level of involvement of an intermediary may vary from simple referrals, for example, solicitors or estate agents making referrals to a specific mortgage or insurance product provider, to fully informed, independent advice and guidance on the appropriate product and product provider. A relatively new channel is the affinity marketing operation. This involves a brand owner with a high-profile brand and a valuable customer database that can be used to promote products or services not currently provided by the brand and database owner. In such circumstances, the product provider supplies products and services under the brand name to the prospective customers on the database on an outsourced basis. The involvement of the brand owner in the product sales and administration will vary according to its own key skills and regulatory requirements.

Many distribution channels are available to promote financial products and services. There are examples of direct and indirect marketing, traditional and e-commerce promotional methods from each category of distributor, product provider, intermediary and affinity operation. What they have in common is their use of personal data to create prospect and customer databases. Such databases are a key asset in any industry; they must be protected and their value maximised by the owner. The use of prospect and customer databases is regulated by data protection law.

A strength of the financial services industry is that it is a largely professional sector, which means that many people who work in the industry will have undergone training with professional bodies such as the Institute of Bankers or the Institute of Actuaries. There are also many professional and industry codes of conduct such as the Banking Code and the Association of British Insurers Code of Practice. Many colleges and universities now offer degrees and other courses in financial services adding a further layer of professionalism which does not rely on, although it might be influenced by, individual employers.

Another strength is that one of the key underlying principles of data protection, confidentiality of personal information, is an acknowledged and familiar concept in the financial services sector. It is a business requirement as well as a legal one and it provides a solid foundation for further training for employees at even the lowest administrative levels about data protection and subject rights.

In Part I of this book each of the data protection principles is considered from the technical aspect. It provides a thorough introduction to the requirements of the Act for those who are unfamiliar with its provisions. It is also a useful reference for those who are already familiar with it and who wish to explore key areas in depth to find solutions to particular problems or to identify the technical requirements behind risk management strategies suggested elsewhere in the book.

In Part II of the book the principles are applied to common aspects of financial services. The key stages in a typical customer life cycle and the data protection issues they raise are considered, starting with advertising messages and working through elements of customer administration and relationship management. Each chapter incorporates suggested risk management strategies for the compliance issue identified and provides a checklist of other principles that apply but that have not been covered in depth.

Part III of the book describes the regulatory environment, describing the role of the Information Commissioner, the regulator for data protection, and the FSA. It concludes with a chapter on the potential for conflict between laws and regulations and how these are accommodated.

CHAPTER 2

Definitions

An understanding of the technical definitions is the first step in understanding the provisions of any statute or statutory instrument. In this chapter each of the key definitions in the Data Protection Act 1998 (the Act) is explained and the intricacies of the technical and legal aspects of each is considered. Other key words and phrases that are helpful in reaching an understanding of the data protection principles, but not found in the Act, are also considered. Cross-reference to other definitions within the explanatory text has been minimised where possible.

PERSONAL DATA

Personal data is recorded information that relates to a living person and that can be associated with that person, either from other information in the possession of the organisation holding the data or by cross-referencing to information held by a third party.

Examples of personal data include:

- details and histories of private customer bank accounts

- details and histories of residential mortgages

- shopping habits and purchase histories relating to store cards, loyalty cards, credit and debit cards

- images caught on closed circuit television (CCTV) systems in shops and branches

- pension records

- insurance policy details

- employment records held by employers, including opinions of line managers, and so on

- tax and national insurance (NI) records held by the Inland Revenue

- medical and dental records

- records of eyesight and eye problems held by opticians

- details of household gas and electricity consumption held by utility companies

- details of property and property owners held by the local council

- vehicle ownership and driver's licence details held by the Driver and Vehicle Licensing Agency (DVLA)

- names and addresses for direct marketing held by any organisation which sends out marketing material

- membership records maintained by clubs, societies, professional and trade bodies.

The list could go on but it illustrates the breadth of the subject and its impact and importance to individuals in their daily lives.

SPECIFIC INCLUSIONS AND EXCLUSIONS

The definition refers to recorded information, so it covers CCTV images, audio tapes and still photographs as well as more obvious recorded media, computer databases, paper files, imaging and microfiche. Other specific inclusions in the definition of 'personal data' are opinions and any indication of intentions towards the individual who is the subject of the information.

Excluded (by omission) from the definition of personal data is information relating to companies, firms, charities and unincorporated associations. Information about deceased persons is not within the definition of personal data, which specifically refers to 'living persons'. Information about persons who cannot be identified from the data or other information likely to be available to the organisation is not personal data because it must be identifiable with an individual. So, for example, CCTV images that show a subject at a distance, too far away to be identifiable, will not be considered personal data.

DURANT V. FINANCIAL SERVICES AUTHORITY

There is now case law on the definition of personal data. It was dramatically affected by the case of *Durant* v. *Financial Services Authority*[1] on appeal in December 2003. The reason its impact was so dramatic was that there had been no significant consideration of the definition in the Courts previously and interpretation was wholly based on the published opinion of the Information Commissioner. This opinion was that personal data meant any reference to an individual regardless of whether the reference was a key part of the information or simply a passing note of someone's involvement in an incident. Thus, for example, a private client file could contain personal data relating to

---

1   *Durant* v. *Financial Services Authority* [2003] EWCA Civ 1746.

the client but also to any members of staff who had worked on the file and signed a memo or letter.

Following the Durant case, the position is quite different. Mr Durant was a customer of Barclays Bank who lost a civil lawsuit involving the bank. He made a complaint to the FSA and surmised that his complaint had been the subject of communication between the FSA and the bank. He then sought to require the FSA to disclose to him such information that he claimed to be personal data under the Act. On appeal, Lord Justice Auld said that the information sought by Mr Durant was not personal data within the meaning of the Act or the EC Directive. His opinion was that the information sought was about the relationship between the bank and its regulator, which included consideration of complaints, that of Mr Durant among them, but which did not have Mr Durant as the focus of the information.

Personal data is now taken to mean information that is biographical in a significant sense. It also means information of which the named individual is the focus. The mere mention of an individual in a record as having been involved in a transaction or event does not constitute personal data. Lord Justice Auld said that whether or not information constituted personal data in any particular instance would depend on how relevant or proximate it was to the individual concerned. The Court held that the mere mention of a named individual does not necessarily constitute their personal data. It considered the reason why data protection law was introduced – to protect privacy – and, with that in mind, it put forward two theories as to what does constitute personal data:

- whether the information is biographical in a significant sense, by which is meant something more than simply recording that a named individual was involved in a matter or event that has no other personal connotations, so that privacy could not be said to have been compromised; and

- whether the named individual is the focus of the information, rather than their involvement in a transaction or event simply being recorded.

The court said: 'In short, it is information that affects his privacy, whether in his personal or family life, business or professional capacity.'

The Durant case has had a significant effect on what we mean by 'personal data' in the UK. The Information Commissioner welcomed the decision and the clarity that it brings to our data protection law;[2] however, the case has raised issues at the EU level, in that there is concern that the law as it stands in the UK may no longer

2 Information Commissioner's case summary of the *Durant* v. *Financial Services Authority* case issued 17 December 2003 and amended 5 October 2004.

meet the requirements of the EC Directive on Data Protection. This matter is under investigation by the EC. If the UK were found to be in breach of its obligation to implement the EC Directive, it would be required to introduce new legislation to reinstate a wider definition of 'personal data' and redress the situation left by the Durant case. Although given our legal status as a member state of the EC, the EC Directive applies directly to personal data processing activity in the UK and is enforceable by the UK courts and the European Court of Justice. Nevertheless, the accepted position in the UK is based on the Durant ruling as UK courts will follow that precedent.

TECHNICAL DEFINITION OF PERSONAL DATA

Section 1(1) of the Data Protection Act 1998 defines data as:

> *information which –*
> a) *is being processed by means of equipment operating automatically in response to instructions given for that purpose,*
> b) *is recorded with the intention that it should be processed by means of such equipment,*
> c) *is recorded as part of a relevant filing system or with the intention that it should form part of a relevant filing system, or*
> d) *does not fall within paragraph (a), (b) or (c) but forms part of an accessible record as defined by section 68.*

Data therefore is information that is processed automatically. This includes information held on personal computers, in programmed telephones and fax machines, on microfiche and imaged documents. It is also information forming or intended to form part of a relevant filing system, which potentially includes paper in filing cabinets, paper on desks, paper in archive, diaries and address books, 'little black books' and rolladex, index card files. It may also be an accessible record that is a health record, an educational record or an accessible public record, all of which are defined terms considered below.

Section 1(1) then defines personal data as data:

> *which relate to a living individual who can be identified –*
> *(a) from those data, or*
> *(b) from the data and other information which is in the possession of, or is likely to come into the possession of, the data controller*
> *and includes any expression of opinion about the individual and any indication of the intentions of the data controller or any other person in respect of the individual.*

The elements of the definition are:

- personal data relates to a living individual, not a company or charity or club

- the individual must be identifiable either from the data or from other information to which the data controller has access.

The second part of the definition is the one that causes most problems. Information that identifies the data subject can be interpreted variously to mean:

- Information can only be personal data if it can identify an individual. This approach allows anonymisation of personal data to break the link between an identifiable individual and information relating to them.

- Information that relates to an identifiable individual but that might not identify them but simply relate to them. Context is important in determining the relevance of the data to the data subject. Overall this is a much more inclusive approach than the first one.

- Information that both clearly identifies and clearly affects the individual. The 'effect' referred to must be on the individual's privacy. This is the approach based on the ruling in the Durant case.

An area where the issue of identification of the individual from the data can be a problem is in relation to CCTV images. If CCTV cameras record images of the general public, these will most likely not be identifiable only from the images themselves and other information in the control of the CCTV scheme operator. However, even after the Durant case, CCTV images are deemed to be 'personal data'. One reason for this is that the EC Directive specifically refers to CCTV images as personal data.[3] Another consideration is that CCTV images are usually recorded for the purpose of crime investigation and criminal prosecution of offenders; therefore the underlying objective is to identify persons shown in the footage.

DATA SUBJECT

This is the individual to whom personal data relates. A data subject need not be a UK national. Any data relating to a living individual that is processed in the UK is subject to the provisions of the Act. This applies whether the individual is British, an EC citizen or located in a territory outside of the European Economic Area (EEA); for example, an underwriter based in the UK may process personal data relating to individuals located in the USA. Those individuals are data subjects under the Act and enjoy the benefit of UK data protection standards even though those standards are potentially higher than those that apply in their home jurisdiction.

---

3   EC Directive 95/46/EC, Recital 16.

In a business context, data subjects include private clients and consumers, trustees, claimants, beneficiaries, employees of the data controller and employees of other organisations such as suppliers and corporate clients. Note that a sole trader will be a data subject and information regarding their business is personal data because there is no legal entity separate from that individual for the data to attach to.

TECHNICAL DEFINITION OF DATA SUBJECT

The Act states:

> *'data subject' means an individual who is the subject of personal data.*

This is reinforced by the judgment in the Durant case that being the focus of the information is a necessary part of the definition. In other words, the individual must be central to the information held and not just a mere bystander whose name is mentioned in a record in passing.

DATA CONTROLLER

The data controller is the party (organisation, company, club or individual) that makes decisions about the personal data to be processed. It decides the purposes for which personal data is to be processed, what personal data is required and how it is obtained.

A trading company is a data controller of personal data connected with the business, its customers and suppliers. An employing company is data controller of employee personal data. Trustees of a pension scheme are the data controller of personal data relating to past and present members of a pension scheme and their dependants. A charity is the data controller of membership and subscriber lists. A club is the data controller of personal data of its members, and so on.

TECHNICAL DEFINITION OF DATA CONTROLLER

Section 1(1) of the Act provides:

> *'data controller' means ... a person who (either alone or jointly or in common with other persons) determines the purposes for which and the manner in which any personal data are, or are to be, processed.*

The elements of the definition are:

● The data controller is the party that determines the purposes for which and the manner in which personal data are processed. This is indicative of control over personal data. Note that data protection law never concerns itself with concepts of 'ownership' of data. The key element is control; the data controller is the party that, either on its own or jointly with another data controller, makes decisions about the processing of personal data. So, for example, an employer that outsources payroll administration is a data controller because it gives instructions to the payroll service provider about the administration of the payroll, such as the names of those who are to receive salary, on what basis and subject to what timings.

● Two or more bodies may be data controllers in relation to the same personal data. In the example of processing personal data for payroll administration purposes, the Inland Revenue and the NI Contributions Agency both operate as data controllers in relation to payroll data (including personal data) supplied by the employer. Employer, Inland Revenue and NI Contributions Agency all process personal data as data controllers and for different purposes.

PROCESSING

'Processing' is used in a very wide sense in relation to data protection. It includes obtaining, using, holding and destroying and deleting personal data. Basically 'processing' means anything that might be done to or with data.

TECHNICAL DEFINITION OF PROCESSING

Section 1(1) of the Act provides:

> *'processing', in relation to information or data, means obtaining, recording or holding the information or data or carrying out any operation or set of operations on the information or data, including –*
>
> *(a) organisation, adaptation or alteration of the information or data,*
> *(b) retrieval, consultation or use of the information or data,*
> *(c) disclosure of the information or data by transmission, dissemination or otherwise making available, or*
> *(d) alignment, combination, blocking, erasure or destruction of the information or data.*

DATA PROCESSOR

A data processor is an organisation that processes personal data on behalf of the data controller. It provides a service in which it has no interest except the payment it receives for carrying out the work.

A data processor may be one of a group of companies. Data protection law does not recognise trading groups of companies; each corporate entity is viewed as a separate data controller and all other corporate entities are 'third parties' despite ownership in common or branding issues. As a consequence, if staff are employed by a service company in a trading group, the service company is necessarily a data processor and the trading companies are data controllers.

Taking the example of a payroll service provider, the data controller is the employer as outlined above (see the definition of 'data controller') and the service provider processes personal data on behalf of the data controller. The data processor, in this example the payroll service provider, has no interest in the data except that it is remunerated by the data controller for carrying out the processing activity. The activities carried out by the data processor are wholly based on the instructions given by the data controller.

TECHNICAL DEFINITION OF DATA PROCESSOR

Section 1(1) of the Act reads:

> *'Data processor', in relation to personal data, means any person (other than an employee of the data controller) who processes the data on behalf of the data controller.*

A key point in this definition is that employees of the data controller are specifically excluded from the definition. Employees are within the authority of the data controller for data protection purposes, unless they commit some act outside of that authority.

EUROPEAN ECONOMIC AREA

The EEA consists of EU member states and Iceland, Liechtenstein and Norway:

- **Current EU member states**: Austria, Belgium, Cyprus, Czech Republic, Denmark, Estonia, Finland, France, Germany, Greece, Hungary, Ireland, Italy, Latvia, Lithuania, Luxembourg, Malta, the Netherlands, Poland, Portugal, Slovakia, Slovenia, Spain, Sweden and the UK.

Up-to-date lists are held on the Information Commissioner's website: www.dataprotection.gov.uk

RELEVANT FILING SYSTEM

This definition relates only to paper files and determines whether or not they are covered by data protection law. The Act states that information is 'personal data' if it is processed, or intended to be processed, by electronic means or if it forms part of a relevant filing system.

The Courts have determined that 'relevant filing system' is to be interpreted narrowly. Paper files form part of a relevant filing system only if they are in a system that provides the same or similar accessibility as a computer filing system. Therefore there must be some external indicator of where relevant information is likely to be held, for example an index or clear labelling.

Even if the filing system appears to be one that provides easy accessibility either by indexation or clear labelling, there is a further requirement. The filing system must allow the identification at the outset of whether a file or set of files within the system contains information relating to a specific data subject. So a system that is indexed might pass the first part of the definition but if in practice the system has not been properly maintained and files are out of order, then it is unlikely to meet the second criteria and will not fall within the definition of a 'relevant filing system'.

This two-part test also applies to individual files within the filing system. To meet the definition, the file must be structured so that a user may identify at the outset that the file contains relevant information and it must be structured so as to allow the user to locate the relevant information quickly.

This definition of 'relevant filing system' is taken from the landmark legal case, *Durant* v. *Financial Services Authority*. 'Relevant filing system' was originally intended to include only some paper files. In practice the definition became almost redundant as the Information Commissioner consistently put forward the view that all paper files should be viewed as being within a 'relevant filing system'. The Durant case has brought clarity to this area of data protection law and the impact is such that probably all paper archive filing is now outside the definition of personal data.

THE TECHNICAL DEFINITION OF RELEVANT FILING SYSTEM

Section 1(1) provides:

> *'Relevant filing system' means any set of information relating to individuals to the extent that, although the information is not processed by means of equipment operating automatically in response to instructions given for that purpose, the set is structured, either by reference to individuals or by reference to criteria relating to individuals,*

> *in such a way that specific information relating to a particular individual is readily accessible.*

In December 2003, in the Durant case, the Court of Appeal of England and Wales ruled on the meaning of 'relevant filing system'. It ruled that whether personal data in a manual filing system fell within the scope of the Act depended upon whether the information was structured in such a way that specific information relating to a particular individual was readily accessible.

Delivering the judgment, Lord Justice Auld said that the Court of Appeal was concerned about the burden of the data protection regime on business. The Court considered that the Data Protection Act 1998 was intended to apply to paper files only if they were of sufficient sophistication to provide 'the same or similar ready accessibility as a computerised filing system. That requires a filing system so referenced or indexed' that a person looking for personal data is able 'to identify at the outset of his search with reasonable certainty and speed the file or files in which the specific data relating to the person requesting the information is located and to locate the relevant information about him within the file or files, without having to make a manual search of them.'[4]

The Court ruled that the mere fact that files are organised chronologically or alphabetically by name does not make a filing system relevant. Although an individual file might be easily identifiable as containing relevant information, the information must also be readily accessible within the file.

NOTIFICATION

Notification is not a defined term but arises from Part III of the Act entitled 'Notification by data controllers'. Section 18 provides that any data controller wishing to be included on the Data Protection Register shall give a notification to the Information Commissioner.

'Notification' means arranging for an entry on the Data Protection Register showing the name of the organisation involved in processing personal data, the purposes for which personal data is processed, and the categories of personal data processed. If the notification regulations require an organisation to register, then processing without registration is prohibited.

---

4   *Durant* v. *Financial Services Authority* [2003] EWCA Civ 1746, Auld, L.J., transcript, p. 21.

SAFE HARBOR

This is a scheme in the USA whereby organisations formally agree to follow a set of data protection principles and guidance. It is regulated by the US Department of Commerce and participation has the approval by the EC as offering an adequate level of protection for the transfer of personal data to US organisations that have signed up to the scheme.

SENSITIVE DATA

A plain English interpretation cannot add to the technical definition which is set out in section 2 of the Act and provides that:

> *Sensitive personal data means personal data consisting of information as to:*
>
> a) *The racial or ethnic origin of the data subject,*
> b) *His political opinions,*
> c) *His religious beliefs or other beliefs of a similar nature,*
> d) *Whether he is a member of a trade union (within the meaning of the Trade Union and Labour Relations (Consolidation) Act 1992),*
> e) *His physical or mental health or condition,*
> f) *His sexual life,*
> g) *The commission or alleged commission by him of any offence, or*
> h) *Any proceedings for any offence committed or alleged to have been committed by him, the disposal of such proceedings or the sentence of any court in such proceedings.*

This is an exclusive definition. No other classes of data are 'sensitive' data.

THIRD PARTY

This term is used in the Act to denote a person or organisation other than a data controller, data processor or the data subject. Employees of data controllers and data processors are not third parties because they are viewed as the operatives of their employer.

ACCESSIBLE RECORD

Section 68 of the Act provides that:

(1) *In this Act 'Accessible record' means –*

   (a) *a health record as defined by subsection (2),*

   (b) *an educational record as defined by Schedule 11, or*

   (c) *an accessible public record as defined by Schedule 12.*

(2) *In subsection (1)(a) 'health record' means any record which –*

   (a) *consists of information relating to the physical or mental health or condition of an individual, and*

   (b) *has been made by or on behalf of a health professional in connection with the care of that individual.*

Schedule 11 provides the definition of an education record but it relates exclusively to schools. It does not cover continuing professional development records or other records maintained of employee training.

Pursuant to section 69, a 'health professional' means any of the following:

   a) *a registered medical practitioner (a 'registered medical practitioner' includes any person who is provisionally registered under section 15 or 21 of the Medical Act 1983 and is engaged in such employment as is mentioned in subsection (3) of that section),*

   b) *a registered dentist as defined by section 53(1) of the Dentists Act 1984,*

   c) *a registered optician as defined by section 36(1) of the Opticians Act 1989,*

   d) *a registered pharmaceutical chemist as defined by section 24(1) of the Pharmacy Act 1954 or a registered person as defined by Article 2(2) of the Pharmacy (Northern Ireland) Order 1976,*

   e) *a registered nurse, midwife or health visitor,*

   f) *a registered osteopath as defined by section 41 of the Osteopaths Act 1993,*

   g) *a registered chiropractor as defined by section 43 of the Chiropractors Act 1994,*

   h) *any person who is registered as a member of a profession to which the Professions Supplementary to Medicine Act 1960 for the time being extends,*

   i) *a clinical psychologist, child psychotherapist or speech therapist,*

   j) *a music therapist employed by a health service body, and*

   k) *a scientist employed by such a body as head of department.*

TABLE OF DEFINITION SOURCES IN THE DATA PROTECTION ACT 1998

Taken from section 71: Index of defined expressions:

Defined expression	Section number
Accessible record	68
Address (in Part III)	16(3)
Business	70(1)
The Commissioner	70(1)
Credit reference agency	70(1)
Data	1(1)
Data controller	1(1) and (4)
Data processor	1(1), (4) and 63(3)
The Data Protection Directive	70(1)
Data protection principles	4 and Schedule 1
Data subject	1(1)
Disclosing (of personal data)	1(2)(b)
EEA State	70(1)
Enactment	70(1)
Enforcement notice	40(1)
Government department	70(1)
Health professional	69
Inaccurate (in relation to data)	70(2)
The non-disclosure provisions (in Part IV)	27(3)
Notification regulations (in Part III)	16(2)
Obtaining (of personal data)	1(2)(a)
Personal data	1(1)
Processing (of information or data)	1(1) and para. 5 of Schedule 8
Recipient (in relation to personal data)	70(1)
Recording (of personal data)	1(2)(a)
Relevant filing system	1(1)
Sensitive personal data	2
The subject information provisions (in Part IV)	27(2)
Third party (in relation to processing of personal data)	70(1)
Using (of personal data)	1(2)(b)

CHAPTER 3

The First Principle

INTERPRETATION

Personal data shall be processed fairly and lawfully, and in particular, shall not be processed unless –

(a) at least one of the conditions in Schedule 2 is met, and

(b) in the case of sensitive personal data, at least one of the conditions in Schedule 3 is also met.

The first data protection principle requires data controllers to process personal data fairly and in accordance with any relevant law. In addition to the general duty to process personal data fairly and lawfully, data controllers must meet specified requirements, otherwise their personal data processing will not be deemed fair.

The first of these specified requirements is that the purpose for which personal data is being processed must meet one or more of the conditions for fair processing set out in a schedule to the Data Protection Act 1998 (the Act). In addition, if sensitive data is being processed (that is data relating to health, race or ethnic origin, membership of a trade union, religious or political beliefs, sex life or criminal records), the purpose for which it is being processed must meet one or more of the conditions for fair processing of sensitive data, also set out in a schedule to the Act.

The second specific requirement for processing to be fair is that data subjects must be given certain information about the data controller and the purposes for which personal data is to be processed.

In summary there are three aspects of fair processing under the first principle. These are:

- the general duty to process fairly and lawfully
- the requirement to meet one or more of the conditions for fair processing
- the requirement to supply subject information.

Each of these aspects is considered in turn below.

THE GENERAL DUTY TO PROCESS FAIRLY AND LAWFULLY

When deciding whether or not a data controller is processing fairly, the Information Commissioner will look at the facts of the case and decide whether or not the processing was fair in relation to that particular case as well as whether or not the processing was generally fair.

This is important because it is possible for processing generally to be fair but in one case where procedures are not followed properly, a particular person might not be treated fairly. For example, an employee in a telephone-based operation with a scripted subject information statement might omit to outline the purposes for which personal data is obtained during one telephone conversation with a consumer. The organisation will be able to show that its procedures include the scripted statement and that staff are trained to deliver the full statement clearly; however, an audio recording of the specific conversation will reveal that the statement was not delivered on that one occasion to that one data subject. Therefore in relation to that one data subject, any subsequent processing of their personal data is unfair because they were not given the statement of subject information prior to being asked to supply any personal data. This is what is known as a 'subjective test'.

HOW IS FAIRNESS ASSESSED?

The Information Commissioner has expressed the view that, in assessing fairness, paramount consideration must be given to the consequences of the processing to the interests of the data subject. This view has been supported by the Data Protection Tribunal.[1]

Some of the questions the Information Commissioner will ask when assessing fairness are:

- Was the person supplying the data under the impression that it would be kept confidential by the data controller and was that impression justified by the circumstances?

- Was any unfair pressure used to obtain the information? Were any unjustified threats or inducements made or offered?

- Was the person improperly led to believe that they must supply the information, or that failure to provide it might disadvantage them?

---

1   *CCN Systems Limited and CCN Credit Systems Limited* v. *The Data Protection Registrar* [1991] DA/90 25/49/9
and *Infolink* v. *The Data Protection Registrar* [1993] DA/90 25/49/9.

As noted above, the test is subjective. The impressions of the data subject are the key criteria. There is a significant overlap with the statutory duty to provide the data subject with prescribed information as to the identity of the data controller and its purposes in obtaining the personal data. The 1984 Act did not include the requirement for data controllers to supply subject information and the Data Protection Registrar (former title of the Information Commissioner) implied the requirement to make it standard in guidance.[2]

LAWFUL PROCESSING

Personal data must be processed in accordance with any relevant legal requirements, both civil and criminal. For example, if personal data is processed under a duty of confidentiality such as exists throughout the financial services sector, the disclosure of that personal data in breach of the duty of confidentiality will be unlawful. Similarly if a contract includes a provision that personal data will not be retained for longer than a specified period, a party to the contract that retains the data beyond the specified period will be processing personal data unlawfully simply by failure to delete the data, independently of whether or how the data is used. Similarly, in relation to employment law, processing payroll information to make unauthorised deductions from salary would constitute unlawful processing.

An important development in relation to lawful processing is the Human Rights Act 1998, which sets out various rights for individuals including the right to respect for the privacy of family life, home and correspondence.[3] Data protection and human rights legislation may work together to increase the protection afforded to individuals. For example, monitoring staff at work without due attention to Article 8 of the Human Rights Act may result in personal data processing that is unlawful and therefore in breach of the Data Protection Act.

THE REQUIREMENT TO MEET ONE OR MORE OF THE CONDITIONS FOR FAIR PROCESSING

The EC Directive on Data Protection sets out the conditions for fair processing of personal data[4] and these have been incorporated into UK law as a requirement of the first principle. The conditions for fair processing of personal data are set out in Schedule 2 of the Act, and personal data processing must meet at least one of those conditions in order to be 'fair' by data protection standards. The conditions for fair

---

2 Information Commissioner (1994) *The Data Protection Principles: (Third Series)* Guideline 4. London: Data Protection Registrar.
3 Human Rights Act 1998, Article 8.
4 EC Directive 95/46/EC, Article 7.

processing of personal data are set out in summary in the table below, and are then considered in detail with examples of how they apply in relation to business activities.

Condition	Comment
Consent	Guidance from the Information Commissioner suggests that consent should be relied upon only as a last resort. Other applicable conditions should be considered first. There are inherent problems with consent, not least that the organisation must be able to deal with those who do not consent and those who change their minds. Also consent is not reliable in the human resources (HR) context.
Contractual obligations where the contract is with the data subject	This covers many circumstances in business where personal data is processed in relation to a contract or steps preparatory to entering into a contract with the data subject such as providing a quote or dealing with an enquiry.
Legal obligations	This covers many non-contractual obligations, for example in relation to health and safety, disclosure to regulators or under statutory obligations to the Inland Revenue, the Department for Social Security (DSS), the Child Support Agency, and so on.
Vital interests of the data subject	Rarely used – 'a matter of life or death'.
Administration of justice and government	Rarely applicable to routine business activities.
Legitimate interests of the data controller or a third party	Where the interests of the data controller or third party are deemed to outweigh any possible harm to the data subject. A useful condition to legitimise marketing activities that are not obviously covered by any other of the conditions. Similarly this is the condition to rely on in relation to takeovers, mergers and acquisitions.

CONSENT

There is no definition of consent in the Act, but the EC Directive[5] defines consent with three key elements:

- It must be freely given.

- It must be specific and informed, so that all processing activity is described.

- It must constitute an indication that the data subject signifies their agreement; inaction will not suffice.

In general, consent to personal data processing activities is not required under current data protection law. There are occasions when it might be necessary if no other authority applies; for example if sensitive data is being processed (see below) or where no other condition for fair processing applies. Consent may also be needed if personal data is to be transferred to a country outside the EEA where adequate standards of data protection do not exist (see Chapter 11 on the eighth principle and transfer of personal data outside the EEA).

Guidance from the Information Commissioner indicates that consent should be the last resort; other conditions to legitimise personal data processing should investigated first.[6] This view is derived from the three-part definition of consent put forward in the EC Directive. First, there is the issue of consent being freely given. When an individual is dealing with a business organisation, particularly a large organisation, there is pressure on the individual to treat on the organisation's standard terms of business. How many consumers successfully challenge standard terms, even where these relate to 'our absolute authority to process your personal data in whatever way we see fit'? And is not the likely response 'take it or leave it' if they do make a challenge? There is unequal bargaining power between an individual and an organisation. It may not amount to duress but it will certainly influence whether or not the organisation is able to establish that consent was freely given. Nowhere else is this so evident than in the relationship between employer and employee.

In the employer/employee relationship it is now doubtful that proper consent can be given by the employee to the processing of personal data relating to them by the employer. The view has been expressed that in the relationship between employer and employee, the employee is at such a disadvantage in terms of bargaining power, that they cannot ever give consent freely and without undue influence from the employer,

---

5   EC Directive 95/46/EC, Article 3(h).
6   Information Commissioner (2001) *The Data Protection Act 1998: Legal Guidance*, para. 3.1.5. London: Data Protection Registrar.

simply by virtue of the fact that this is the employer. The Information Commissioner indicated agreement with this view.[7]

Second, as noted above, consent is not a prerequisite to personal data processing. The legal requirement, as set out in the interpretive provisions relating to the first principle, is for data subjects to be given information about personal data processing activity before they supply any personal data. In theory at least, on the basis of information provided pursuant to the first principle the data subject can choose whether or not to supply personal data in the first place. Thus consent is not ordinarily an appropriate condition to meet the fair processing conditions of the first principle.

Finally, there are logistical issues with reliance on consent as authority to process personal data. Some data subjects might not consent when presented with a choice. Other data subjects might withdraw their consent at a later stage. So, if the organisation relies on consent to legitimise personal data processing, it needs a procedure to deal with those data subjects who refuse or later revoke their consent.

In relation to the requirement for consent to be indicated by a positive act, the Information Commissioner has stated[8] that a data subject may signify consent other than in writing so long as there is some active communication between the parties.

MEETING CONTRACTUAL OBLIGATIONS

The second condition in Schedule 2 relates to processing necessary for the performance of a contract to which the data subject is a party. This is the condition that is favoured for customer or client personal data processing. The data subject is party to a contract for a mortgage product, a savings scheme or account, insurance or investments. The administration of those products is undertaken pursuant to the contract between the parties and one of the parties is the data subject.

This contractual condition also includes processing necessary for the taking of steps at the request of the data subject with a view to entering into a contract. This covers pre-contractual processing activity, for example when personal data is supplied to a broker and disclosed onwards to product providers for purposes of obtaining quotes and product illustrations. These are steps preliminary to entering into a contract with

---

7   In an Opinion (8/2001, September 2001) issued by the Article 29 Working Party (advisory group to EC on data protection matters) it was suggested that where the employer is required to process personal data for 'necessary and unavoidable' purposes associated with employment administration, it would be misleading if the employer were to seek to rely on consent from the employee to legitimise the resultant personal data processing activities. The view expressed was that consent by an employee cannot be demonstrated to have been freely given to the employer because of the risk of prejudice to the employee's continued employment and prospects at work. The Information Commissioner has concurred with this view.

8   *Legal Guidance*, para. 3.1.5.

the data subject, even where the data subject then declines to enter into the contract on the terms offered.

MEETING LEGAL OBLIGATIONS OF THE DATA CONTROLLER

The third condition recognises processing necessary for compliance with any legal obligation to which the data controller is subject, other than an obligation imposed by contract. This condition legitimises personal data processing undertaken for purposes largely unrelated to the data subject, as it recognises the other legal obligations to which a data controller may be subject. A prime example would be reporting to a regulatory authority or disclosure of personal data to relevant authorities as part of money laundering prevention measures. It also includes processing of personal data for health and safety purposes.

Many legal obligations are imposed by statute. Strictly speaking the data controller should comply with a statutory requirement only to the extent that is authorised by the statute in question; for example an enquiry made under a statutory authority must comply with the limits outlined in the statute. So an enquiry about a specific data subject should not be framed in such as way as to seek to elicit personal data relating to another data subject, a partner for example. However, it is not often that an administrator has the expertise to evaluate the limits of a statutory authority and to determine whether or not a given enquiry falls within that authority.

PROTECTING THE VITAL INTERESTS OF THE DATA SUBJECT

This condition applies where processing is necessary to protect the vital interests of the data subject. This has been interpreted by the Information Commissioner to mean a 'life or death' situation[9] and is not generally particularly useful in routine business operations although there could be circumstances involving the health of an employee.

THE ADMINISTRATION OF JUSTICE AND GOVERNMENT FUNCTIONS

The fifth condition relates to the administration of justice and Crown and public functions and is unlikely to apply generally to business activities except perhaps in relation to personnel administration. It will cover situations where personal data must be processed as part of a police investigation for example, or it might be quoted as applying to information required by the Child Support Agency. Equally these disclosures would be covered by the condition which recognises processing necessary to meet a legal obligation of the data controller.

---

9   *Legal Guidance,* para. 3.1.1

It also covers the exercise of any other functions of a public nature exercised in the public interest by any person. This would apply to processing undertaken on behalf of directors, officers or staff members who have a public role, for example chairperson or committee member of a professional institute or charitable work.

LEGITIMATE INTERESTS

This condition applies where personal data processing is in the legitimate interests of the data controller or a third party and does not prejudice the rights and freedoms of the data subject in relation to their personal data. The necessary components to establish processing pursuant to this condition are:

- it should be in the legitimate interests

- of the data controller or third parties to whom the data are disclosed

- balanced against the rights and freedoms and legitimate interests of the data subject.

This is a catch-all to a large extent and covers processing that can neither be brought within the aegis of contract nor any other legal duty imposed on the data controller. It is qualified to the extent that the data controller should balance its own legitimate interests against the rights of the data subjects.

The Information Commissioner has suggested a two-part test to establish whether the 'legitimate interests' condition is appropriate in any particular case. The first part is to consider the legitimacy of the interests pursued by the data controller or third party. The second part is to consider the rights and freedoms or legitimate interests of the data subject and decide whether or not these are prejudiced by the processing activities of the data controller and, if so, whether the data subject's interests override those of the data controller.

A key area where this will apply is in relation to marketing activity. There is no other obvious justification for processing personal data for marketing purposes except that it is in the legitimate interests of the data controller. There are additional safeguards for the rights and freedoms of data subjects in relation to the use of personal data for marketing purposes. There is a statutory right to object to the use of personal data for direct marketing purposes and the current requirement to meet subject information provisions in relation to any marketing involves an opt-out clause as a minimum. To a large extent therefore the rights and freedoms of individuals in relation to their personal information is protected in relation to marketing activity. The use of personal information for marketing purposes therefore is a legitimate interest of the data controller with adequate safeguards for the rights of data subjects.

There is provision for the Home Secretary to specify particular circumstances in which the sixth condition is, or is not, to be taken to be satisfied. To date no order has been made pursuant to this clause.

MEETING ONE OR MORE OF THE CONDITIONS FOR FAIR PROCESSING OF SENSITIVE DATA

Processing involving sensitive data must meet one of the conditions for fair processing of personal data as well as one of the following conditions for fair processing of sensitive data. Note that conditions from both lists must be met.

Sensitive data means personal data consisting of information as to:

a) *The racial or ethnic origin of the data subject,*

b) *His political opinions,*

c) *His religious beliefs or other beliefs of a similar nature,*

d) *Whether he is a member of a trade union (within the meaning of the Trade Union and Labour Relations (Consolidation) Act 1992),*

e) *His physical or mental health or condition,*

f) *His sexual life,*

g) *The commission or alleged commission by him of any offence, or*

h) *Any proceedings for any offence committed or alleged to have been committed by him, the disposal of such proceedings or the sentence of any court in such proceedings.*

The conditions that legitimise processing of sensitive data as fair are laid out in the following table, and then explained in detail.

Condition	Comment
Explicit consent	Unreliable for reasons explained above in relation to ordinary consent. Note that the standard required is for 'explicit' consent rather than simple consent required for fair processing of ordinary personal data.
Meeting legal obligations in connection with employment	This includes processing to meet the requirements of statutory sick pay (SSP), Inland Revenue and Benefits Agency requirements. It might include legal obligations in relation to other employees, for example, disclosure of details of infectious illness of one employee so that other employees can take preventive measures.
Vital interests of the data subject	Rarely used, a matter of 'life or death'.
Non-profit-making bodies	Not applicable to businesses.
Information already in the public domain	This cannot apply generally but only in relation to specific instances.
Legal rights	The establishment or defence of the legal rights of the data controller, for example, discussing dismissal of an employee for absence through sickness with a solicitor.
Administration of justice and government	Not generally useful in a business context.
Medical purposes	Relates to processing undertaken by a 'health professional'.
Equal opportunities monitoring	Restricted to use where equal opportunities are promoted, not otherwise.

EXPLICIT CONSENT

This condition requires the data subject to give explicit consent to the processing. There is no definition of 'explicit consent' in the Act, but it is reasonable to assume that the requirement is more rigorous than simple 'consent'. As outlined above, businesses are advised not to rely on consent as a condition to establish fair processing because of the need to establish that consent is freely given, without duress, and unless it is able to handle those situations where a data subject declines to give their consent.

Guidance from the Information Commissioner states that 'explicit' consent suggests that the consent of the data subject should be absolutely clear.[10] It is suggested that the category of sensitive data, and the proposed purpose for which it will be processed, must be stated in subject information for a data subject to give explicit consent to that use.

MEETING LEGAL OBLIGATIONS IN CONNECTION WITH EMPLOYMENT

This condition applies where processing is necessary for the purposes of exercising or performing any right or obligation which is conferred or imposed by law on the data controller in connection with employment.

Obviously this will be a useful condition in the human resources (HR) context. An example where it might apply is where sensitive data is shared between employer and pension scheme trustees as part of routine liaison and communication, particularly when an employee is likely to retire early due to ill health. The processing is necessary in order to exercise rights and obligations relating to the contract of employment that provides pension scheme membership as part of the employment remuneration package. The pension scheme rules are also likely to provide a legal obligation basis for fair processing of information about the health of the data subject. Another example would be processing sensitive data relating to an accident or injury suffered at work to meet health and safety requirements.

There is provision for the Home Secretary to specify particular cases where this condition may be excluded or to specify further conditions that must be met before the condition can be regarded as satisfied. To date no order has been made pursuant to this clause.

PROTECTING THE VITAL INTERESTS OF THE DATA SUBJECT OR ANOTHER PERSON

This condition applies to processing necessary to protect the vital interests of the data subject. This has been interpreted narrowly by the Information Commissioner to mean a 'life or death' situation and is not generally particularly useful in routine business administration. However, it is not as straightforward in application as its counterpart in Schedule 2 and further qualifications apply.

The processing must be necessary to protect the vital interests of the data subject or another person, in a case where either consent cannot be given by or on behalf of the data subject, or the data controller cannot reasonably be expected to obtain the

10 *Legal Guidance*, para. 3.1.5.

consent of the data subject. Where the contention is that the processing is necessary to protect the vital interests of another person, the data controller can show that consent by or on behalf of the data subject has been unreasonably withheld and legitimately undertake the processing.

NON-PROFIT-MAKING BODIES

This condition applies where the data controller is not established or conducted for profit, and it exists for political, philosophical, religious or trade union purposes. The condition applies so long as personal data processing is carried out in the course of the data controller's legitimate activities, with appropriate safeguards for the rights and freedoms of specific categories of data subject. Furthermore, the processing cannot involve the disclosure of personal data to a third party without the consent of the data subject. The 'specific categories of data subject' referred to are those individuals who either are members of the data controller (for example, members of a club or charity foundation) or have regular contact with it in connection with its purposes.

INFORMATION ALREADY IN THE PUBLIC DOMAIN

This condition provides that information comprising sensitive data that has been made public as a result of steps deliberately taken by the data subject may be processed by the data controller. A prime example of this condition in action occurred in January 2002 when government ministers used the press to publicly reject families' claims that elderly patients had been failed by the National Health Service (NHS) system by being allowed to wear soiled clothing and not having the aftermath of their injuries fully cleaned when in hospital. The rebuttal included sensitive data relating to the elderly patients, explaining that in their distress and confusion they had strongly resisted moves to clean and re-clothe them. This apparent disclosure of sensitive data was already in the public domain, disclosed to the press by the patients and their families. The government rebuttal simply made use of the information already in the public domain.

Consideration should be given to how wide a 'public' is required to establish that sensitive data is in the public domain. For example, personal data might be disclosed to a limited group of individuals without it being in the public domain.

LEGAL RIGHTS

This condition recognises the need for sensitive data to be processed in connection with establishing or defending legal rights. An organisation would rely on this condition when disclosing sensitive data to an insurer in relation to a personal injury liability claim on its insurance. Such a claim is notice that an individual considers it has legal rights enforceable against the data controller. The data controller's defence will involve a claim on its insurance, even though the claim may not conclude in court but be settled on agreed terms between the parties.

This condition includes allowance for processing sensitive data necessary for the purpose of obtaining legal advice where legal proceedings are pending or anticipated.

ADMINISTRATION OF JUSTICE AND GOVERNMENT FUNCTIONS

As with the corresponding condition in Schedule 2, this condition covers processing necessary for the administration of justice, for the exercise of any functions conferred on any person by or under an enactment, or for the exercise of any functions of the Crown, a Minister of the Crown or a government department.

There is provision for the Secretary of State to specify particular cases where this condition may be excluded or to specify further conditions that must be met before the condition can be regarded as satisfied. To date no order has been made pursuant to this clause.

MEDICAL PURPOSES

This condition covers the situation where processing is necessary for medical purposes and is undertaken by a health professional, or a person who, in the circumstances, owes a duty of confidentiality equivalent to that which would arise if that person were a health professional.

For the purposes of this condition 'medical purposes' includes the purposes of preventive medicine, medical diagnosis, medical research, the provision of care and treatment and the management of health care services.

This condition obviously has application in relation to occupational health screening (preventive medicine), and medical insurance, the provision of care and treatment and the management of healthcare services. The condition does not apply to processing in relation to other kinds of insurance or for obtaining personal data in relation to the sale or underwriting of insurance.

EQUAL OPPORTUNITIES MONITORING

This condition applies to processing of information about racial or ethnic origin that is necessary for the purpose of identifying or keeping under review the existence or absence of equality of opportunity or treatment between persons of different racial or ethnic origins. The processing must be undertaken with a view to enabling equality to be promoted or maintained, and must be carried out with appropriate safeguards for the rights and freedoms of data subjects.

There is provision for the Secretary of State to specify particular circumstances in which processing is, or is not, to be taken to provide the appropriate safeguards for the rights and freedoms of data subjects. To date no order has been made pursuant to this clause.

This is an important condition in relation to equal opportunities monitoring although it is worth noting that many employers could rely on the second condition, which would apply to processing necessary for the purposes of exercising or performing any right or obligation that is conferred or imposed by law on the data controller in connection with employment. Equal opportunities monitoring is an obligation imposed by law on certain data controllers.

FURTHER CONDITIONS: THE SENSITIVE DATA ORDER 2000

In addition to the conditions for fair processing of sensitive data set out in Schedule 3 to the Act, there is provision for the Secretary of State to specify additional circumstances in which fair processing of sensitive data may be established. To date one order, The Data Protection (Processing of Sensitive Data) Order 2000 has been made. It provides for fair processing of sensitive data in a variety of circumstances. These are laid out in the following table, and considered in detail below.

Circumstances	*Comment*
Prevention or detection of unlawful acts	Limited in application, requiring substantial public interest rather than simply prevention of crime, which takes it out of contention for most businesses.
Confidential counselling services	Limited in application, also requiring substantial public interest and explicit consent must first have been considered and rejected.
Insurance and pensions	Limited in application, but significant in the life and pensions industry.
Equal opportunities	An obvious condition for HR processing activity, designed for use where equal opportunities are promoted not otherwise.
Political opinions	Limited in application, applies only to political organisations not businesses.
Research	Limited in application, restricted to substantial public interest.
Police	Limited in application, restricted to the police.

Prevention or detection of unlawful acts

There are two similar conditions and they require that processing be in the substantial public interest. Arguably any processing related to the prevention or detection of any unlawful act is in the public interest, but the requirement is that it should be in the 'substantial' public interest so is obviously not intended to be applied to any and all unlawful acts. The provisions are for:

- processing undertaken in circumstances in which the consent of the data subject would prejudice the prevention or detection of the unlawful act;

- processing necessary for the discharge of any function designed to protect the public against dishonesty, malpractice, or other seriously improper conduct by, or the unfitness or incompetence of, any person, or the mismanagement of any body or association.

Confidential counselling services

This condition requires that processing be in the substantial public interest and applies to processing necessary for the discharge of any function that is designed for the provision of confidential counselling, advice, support or any other service. There is a qualification that explicit consent should normally be sought, but this condition will apply if the processing is carried out without the explicit consent of the data subject either because consent would prejudice the provision of the counselling or other advisory or support service, or because consent cannot be given by the data subject or the data controller cannot reasonably be expected to obtain explicit consent.

Insurance business and occupational pension schemes

Conditions have also been established under the Sensitive Data Order to allow fair processing of sensitive data necessary for the purpose of carrying on an insurance business or making determinations in connection with eligibility for, and benefits payable under, an occupational pension scheme. The conditions authorise processing of sensitive data relating to health only if it relates to the parent, grandparent, great-grandparent or sibling of an insured person or member of a pension scheme.

These are essential conditions for medical and insurance underwriters to ascertain the morbidity and mortality risk presented by a proposer based on the health of close family members. Generally, questions about the health of close family members are answered by the proposer and the organisation is denied the opportunity to obtain the explicit consent of the data subjects.

A qualification to the conditions is that the processing must not support measures or decisions made in connection with the data subject. So, sensitive data comprising the medical history of near relatives may be processed for the purposes of assessing the risk posed by an individual making an insurance proposal or being considered for entry into pension scheme membership or benefits. But the same information cannot be processed to make a decision relating to the parent, grandparent, great-grandparent or sibling.

A further qualification is that the processing must be necessary in a case where the data controller cannot reasonably be expected to obtain the explicit consent of the data subject (in this case the parent, grandparent, and so on) and is not aware that the data subject has withheld their consent. So the conditions fit specific circumstances where an individual provides sensitive data relating to family members as part of a proposal for life insurance or membership of a pension scheme. The condition legitimises sensitive data processing in relation to the individual only, not in relation to the data subjects.

Additional condition: Processing to monitor equal opportunities

In the same way as processing of sensitive data relating to race or ethnic origin may be processed fairly to monitor equal opportunities, so may sensitive data relating to religion be processed in order to monitor equal opportunities. Interestingly the Sensitive Data Order also provides for data subjects to prevent such processing by notice to the data controller, effectively creating a new right for data subjects.

Processing sensitive data relating to political opinions

A new condition allows the processing of sensitive data relating to political opinions of data subjects where the processing is undertaken by political organisations and where it does not cause, nor is likely to cause, substantial damage or distress to data subjects or any other person.

There is provision also for data subjects to prevent such processing by notice to the data controller, a new right for data subjects.

Research

Processing that is in the substantial public interest and necessary for research purposes may benefit from another new condition set out in the Sensitive Data Order. The requirements are that the processing does not support measures or decisions with respect to any particular data subject unless the explicit consent of the data subject is obtained in addition and the processing does not cause, nor is likely to cause, substantial damage or distress to the data subject or any other person.

Business research is unlikely to qualify as being in the significant public interest, but some sectors may be able to take advantage of the condition; for example pharmaceutical companies developing new drugs as well as universities and bodies established for research on a non-profit-making basis.

Police

Processing that is necessary for the exercise of any functions conferred on a constable by any rule of law is fair processing under the Sensitive Data Order.

SUMMARY

The EC Directive on Data Protection sets out the conditions for fair processing of personal data and these have been incorporated into UK law as a requirement of the first data protection principle. The conditions are set out in Schedule 2 to the Act and data controllers are required to ensure that personal data processing undertaken by them, or on their behalf, meets one or more of the conditions for fair processing. There is no requirement to specify which condition is relied upon when processing personal data. In practice, the only occasion this will be queried is if a data controller enters into correspondence with the Information Commissioner in connection with a complaint, known as a request for assessment in the parlance of the Act.

Also, in general terms, data controllers are unlikely to have difficulty in establishing that personal data processing meets one or more of the conditions for fair processing set out in Schedule 2. The difficulty arises where the data controller processes sensitive data. The differentiation between personal data and sensitive data is derived directly from the EC Directive, as is the higher degree of compliance requiring data controllers to meet one or more conditions for processing sensitive data set out in Schedule 3 to the Act as well as a condition from Schedule 2.

The conditions for fair processing of sensitive data are considerably more restrictive than those applicable to personal data processing. Significantly, an order was made pursuant to the Act to create additional conditions for fair processing of sensitive data. The Sensitive Data Order 2000 creates very specific conditions to meet the needs of data controllers (including some financial services institutions) who intensively lobbied the Home Office for additional conditions to allow them to continue existing sensitive data processing activities for which Schedule 3 of the Act had omitted to cater.

The restricted grounds for establishing fairness when processing sensitive data is a problem throughout the EC. Most of the Information Commissioners located in different member states report problems with the conditions, and there is discussion about removing the higher level of compliance for fair processing of sensitive data. In the UK this would mean the disapplication of sub-paragraph (b) of the first principle and the entire Schedule 3 list of conditions.

Consent of the data subject is a condition common to both the second and third schedules. It can be seen that consent is not a prerequisite to fair processing, however; many other conditions may apply, particularly in relation to processing personal data rather than sensitive data.

Finally it is worth noting that even where personal data processing activity meets one or more of the conditions for fair processing, it does not follow that the processing is fair. Fairness will also depend on the circumstances of the processing (the subjective test referred to earlier) and on the subject information requirements being met.

RISK MANAGEMENT STRATEGIES

This is an area of data protection law that is largely unseen. Only when an organisation is under investigation in relation to other data protection problems is it asked to declare on which of the conditions for fair processing it seeks to rely when processing personal and sensitive data.

However, the conditions contain many of the elements of data protection law and making an initial assessment of the most likely conditions to apply to any processing activity is a useful activity in the short term, leading to a greater understanding of data protection law. In the longer term it might be an invaluable activity; if the business is dealing with a data protection problem and the issue of conditions for fair processing arises, any advance thoughts on the subject will be helpful. It would be worthwhile to document any initial thoughts on the conditions applicable to personal and sensitive data processing carried on around the organisation.

THE REQUIREMENT TO PROVIDE SUBJECT INFORMATION

The interpretive provisions applying to the first principle require a data controller to provide specified information to data subjects before any personal data is obtained from them. The information required is:

- the identity of the data controller and, if the data controller has nominated a representative for the purposes of the Act, the identity of that representative;

- details of the purposes for which personal data is processed or is intended to be processed;

- any further information which is necessary, having regard to the specific circumstances in which the data are or are to be processed, to enable processing in respect of the data subject to be fair.

THE IDENTITY OF THE DATA CONTROLLER

This is a straightforward requirement and, in practice, the data controller's name usually features on literature where subject information is required. The ideal location for a subject information notice is on any form that purports to gather personal data, such as an account application form, enquiry form, insurance proposal or quotation request form.

Whether or not the full legal title of the data controller is required is not certain; there is no case law or definition to provide guidance. It does seem to be proper to use the full legal title for registered companies, however, as then there can be no doubt as to the identity of the data controller. An advertisement that invites potential customers or clients to submit personal data obviously requires the inclusion of appropriate subject information. Given the pressure on space in advertisements and the widespread emphasis on branding in the financial services sector, a company logo may suffice to communicate the identity of the data controller. Perhaps a key point to consider is whether or not a data subject can identify the data controller from the information provided. If a brand name is used, it should be registered on the Data Protection Register as a business name to facilitate access to the registration by an enquiring data subject.

A share registrar nominated to handle queries from shareholders of the data controller is an example of a representative nominated for the purposes of the Act. The company in which shareholders have chosen to invest is the data controller, the administration of the share register is outsourced to a share registrar service provider and it is practical for queries to be handled direct by the registrar. In these circumstances the registrar can be nominated as representative of the data controller for the purposes of the Act.

THE PURPOSES FOR WHICH THE DATA ARE INTENDED TO BE PROCESSED

These should include a reference to the main processing activity and any ancillary activities. Care needs to be taken to identify all processing activities for inclusion in the wording of the subject information notice.

Marketing is an obvious secondary processing purpose for personal data supplied in connection with a new customer or client account. Other, non-obvious processing purposes should be stated, such as fraud prevention initiatives.

This part of the first principle, taken in conjunction with the second principle, operates to restrict personal data processing activities to those stated in subject information. This can cause significant problems as explained in the next chapter, which looks at the second data protection principle.

ANY OTHER INFORMATION RELEVANT IN THE CIRCUMSTANCES

A good starting point to identify what information could be relevant for inclusion in statements of subject information is to consider if there are any circumstances that would affect the data subject's decision to supply the information requested. This includes:

- details of any third parties to whom the data will be disclosed

- other sources of personal data relating to the data subject

- the consequences of not supplying the information requested

- the period of time during which the personal data will be retained.

So, for example, a subject information notice on an account application form might read:

> *The information requested is required for the purpose of opening and administering an account with Name of Provider Limited. All the information we request is necessary to assist us in opening and administering the account and we may not be able to proceed with your application if you do not answer all the questions. You should be aware that we share information with XYZ Limited for fraud prevention purposes.*

This draft notice covers:

- the identity of the data controller – Name of Provider Limited

- the purposes for which the data will be processed:

  - opening and administering an account

  - fraud prevention measures

- other information relevant in the circumstances:

  - if any of the information requested is not provided we may not be able to process the application

  - we share or disclose information for fraud prevention purposes.

PERSONAL DATA OBTAINED FROM THIRD PARTIES

Where personal data is not obtained direct from the data subject but from a third party, the data controller should provide subject information when they first process the personal data or at the earliest reasonable opportunity. Therefore if a data controller purchases a mailing list, when first contacting prospects on the list, appropriate wording should be included about the data controller's personal data processing activities. Where data is not collected direct from the data subject, the data controller is still under a duty to ensure that appropriate subject information notice is given within a reasonable time of starting processing activity.

A typical arrangement of this type where personal data is sourced from a third party involves standard broking activity. The broker discloses personal data to a range of product providers to obtain quotes for a private client. Documentation from product providers should include their own subject information so that it is made available to the data subject at the first available opportunity.

There are exceptions to the requirement to provide subject information notices where the personal data was obtained from a third party. These apply:

- where providing the subject information would involve disproportionate effort; or

- where the disclosure is one required by law.

If a data controller intends to rely on the disproportionate effort exemption they must record the specific circumstances and the reasons why compliance would involve disproportionate effort. The Information Commissioner would consider factors such as the nature of the data, the resource demands in terms of time and money to provide subject information, these factors being weighed against the prejudice to data subjects of not being provided with subject information.[11]

TIMING OF PROVIDING SUBJECT INFORMATION

The interpretive provisions relating to the Second Principle consider two scenarios, first where the data is obtained from the data subject and second where the data is obtained from a third party. It is not specifically stated that subject information should be provided before personal data is obtained, but the Information Commissioner has always insisted on this. This is sensible, as obtaining personal data direct from the data subject obviously involves some communication between data controller and data subject and therefore provision of subject information is not difficult to achieve. Also as the data subject may make a decision whether or not to supply the data requested on

---

11 *Legal Guidance*, para. 3.1.7.6.

the basis of the data controller's stated processing purposes, it must be provided before any personal data is obtained.

Where personal data is sourced from a third party, the requirement is that subject information be provided before the 'relevant time'. This is either at the time the data controller first processes the data or if disclosure to a third party is envisaged:

- at the time of disclosure; or

- at the time when it became clear that disclosure to a third party was unlikely; or

- at the end of a reasonable period.

PROMINENCE OF SUBJECT INFORMATION – SIZE AND POSITIONING

The Information Commissioner has stated that it would be inappropriate to set down rules about the size, positioning and wording of notification clauses, so it is a matter of judgment; data controllers should keep in mind 'fairness'. The following are questions the Information Commissioner is likely to consider when assessing the adequacy of the prominence given to a notice:

- Is the typeface or font in the notification of at least an equivalent size to the typeface or font used in the rest of the form?

- If not, is the print nevertheless of sufficient size for the data subject's eye to be drawn to it?

- Is the layout and print size such that the notification is easy to read and does not appear cramped?

- Is the notification placed at or very close to the place where the data subject supplies their details or signs the form?

- If not, is it placed in such as way that the data subject will inevitably see it in the course of filling in the form?

- If not, is it nevertheless placed where the data subject's eye will be drawn to it?

- Is the general nature and presentation of the form such that it conveys to the data subject the need to read carefully all the details including the notification clause?

As a general rule, the size of font or typeface used for the notice should be no less prominent than any font or typeface used for any other part of the document.

The location of subject information will depend on the correspondence between data controller and data subject. If a telephone interview is conducted, then a spoken form of words will be required. If applications for a quote are invited online, an appropriate form of words is required on the web page before the data subject submits their enquiry. A paper form with data entry fields should have a written statement at the top of the form or, if space is tight, a statement directing the data subject's attention to the data protection wording elsewhere on the form.

WHAT MAKES AN EFFECTIVE NOTICE?

The following are questions the Information Commissioner is likely to consider when assessing the efficacy of notices:[12]

- Do the words used convey all the likely non-obvious uses and disclosures of the customer's information?

- Do the words properly convey the fact that information about the customer will be passed on to others?

- Do the words convey the full implications for the customer of the use or disclosure, for example that they might receive telephone marketing calls?

- Do the words explain the above in a way that would be understood by the great majority of likely data subjects?

No exemptions from the subject information requirements

There are no significant exemptions from the requirement to supply subject information. Also it should be noted that the subject information provisions take effect to overrule any enactment or rule of law prohibiting or restricting the disclosure, or authorising the withholding of information. The main force of this provision is felt in relation to subject access requests but it makes the point that data protection law overrides many other areas of law and any organisation choosing not to comply with subject information requirements, for example, had better take legal advice on the likely consequences.

RISK MANAGEMENT STRATEGIES

Compliance personnel should take the time to identify how personal data is obtained and its use for business purposes. Having identified how personal data is obtained and the purposes for which it is processed, check that subject information statements are appropriate and that these are included in literature to ensure that every data subject will see or hear the statement prior to being asked to furnish personal data. Remember

---

12 Text taken from the Information Commissioner's website, www.informationcommissioner.gov.uk.

to include a notice on the website if applications and other communication are invited online.

Document how and when reviews are undertaken and any actions resulting from them. This may be useful in future if the organisation is challenged on data protection issues.

Given the importance of subject information and the subjective nature of the test for fair processing to meet the requirements of the first data protection principle, it is recommended that subject information is included in all consumer facing materials that can handle the wording (for example, a press advertisement may have limited space). If an application form is damaged or defaced so as to obliterate the subject information statement, appropriate wording in product literature may help to remedy the fault. The only potential issue here is whether or not statements of subject information are consistent. So the final recommendation is for regular checks for consistency to be carried out.

CHAPTER 4

The Second Principle

Personal data shall be obtained only for one or more specified and lawful purposes and shall not be processed in any manner incompatible with that purpose or those purposes.

INTERPRETATION

The following key elements can be extracted from the text of the second data protection principle:

- personal data must be obtained for specific purposes;

- all purposes for which personal data is processed must be lawful; and

- all processing of personal data must relate to the original purpose or purposes for which it was obtained.

Each of these three elements is considered separately below. Their impact on personal data processing in the business context is assessed and the risk of non-compliance explored with guidance on how to minimise that risk.

PERSONAL DATA MUST BE OBTAINED FOR SPECIFIC PURPOSES

The purposes for which personal data will be processed must be specified at or before the time when the personal data is obtained. In order for this to happen, the purposes for which it is intended that personal data be processed must be predefined. This means an organisation must identify all the likely potential purposes for which personal data might be processed and then ensure that it communicates its intentions in the appropriate ways.

There are two distinct and separate requirements for specifying the organisation's processing intentions and both specifications must be complete and accurate if the organisation is to comply with the principles. First, the organisation's entry in the Data Protection Register includes specified purposes for which personal data will be processed. It is a criminal offence to fail to keep a register entry up to date and accurate in terms of the personal data processing activities of the registrant.[1] Second, the information to be supplied to prospective data subjects (the 'subject information' requirement set out in the first principle) includes the purposes for which it is intended the data be processed. These two statements, the registration entry and the statement of subject information, should be in accordance with one another, although it is likely that the wording used to explain those intentions to the data subject will differ from the wording on the statutory register.

There is an inherent restriction on the organisation's activities arising from the requirement to ensure that these two statements of intention of processing activity, the register entry and subject information, are complete and accurate. The statements provide authority for the organisation to process personal data and its authority is circumscribed by the content of the statement. This creates two potential issues. First, where the organisation has failed to accurately define its processing activity, leaving it without adequate authority for its processing activity. Second, when undertaking 'green field' projects for which the organisation does not have pre-existing authority from its prospect or customer database.

An additional point is that prospect or customer information cannot be sought in the hope that one day it will be useful. At the time of including a prospective processing purpose in subject information and on the register, the organisation must be reasonably convinced that it will so utilise the personal data in the relatively near future. Guidance from the Information Commissioner's Office[2] has indicated that it is not acceptable to obtain and hold information on the basis that it might be useful in the future.

To manage the risks inherent in the second principle organisations should undertake regular audits of their personal data processing activity to ensure that registration entries and statements of subject information are up to date and adequately reflect the actual processing of personal data.

Further, any planned change to personal data processing activities must first be reflected in the register entry and subject information before changes can be implemented. So a bank with a database of information relating to its banking customers should amend its registration and its subject information in advance of utilising personal data, for example, to assess the home insurance risk that individual customers represent. Otherwise it is processing personal data without due authority and in breach of the first and second data protection principles. Planning is the key to compliance in this area and the organisation should ensure that a lawyer or data

1   Act, section 21.
2   *Legal Guidance*, section 3.3 on the third data protection principle (now renumbered as the second principle).

protection expert is available to advise on new projects at any early stage of planning to highlight data protection issues.

ALL PURPOSES FOR WHICH DATA IS PROCESSED MUST BE LAWFUL

This is a restatement of the first data protection principle, which requires that personal data be processed fairly and lawfully. An example of unlawful processing would be disclosure of personal data in breach of a duty of confidentiality. All financial institutions owe their customers a duty of confidentiality following the banking case *Tournier* v. *National Provincial and Bank of England.*[3] To disclose customer personal data in breach of a duty of confidentiality would constitute unlawful processing bearing in mind that the wide definition of 'processing' includes disclosure.

ALL PROCESSING MUST RELATE TO THE ORIGINAL PURPOSE OR PURPOSES FOR WHICH DATA WAS OBTAINED

The first and second principles work in harmony. The first principle requires that individuals be given prescribed information before any personal data is obtained. The prescribed information includes the purposes for which the data is intended to be processed. If the purposes are not determined at the time of obtaining the data, individual data subjects are not given adequate subject information and the organisation is left without due authority to process the personal data obtained.

The second principle requires the purposes for which personal data are obtained to be specified and any future processing has to be carried out in accordance with that specification. So, unless data subjects are advised of the intentions of the organisation both in relation to existing processing purposes and new developments that involve processing personal data for other, different, purposes, the second principle prevents any processing for the new, different, purposes.

In practice this may not be unduly restrictive for routine business developments. The wording of subject information statements should permit slight variations in the processing of personal data. The overriding purpose for which personal data is processed, for example in connection with the provision of banking services, allows generous interpretation. So, a bank or building society offering a new deposit product, for example, will not be restricted in terms of using existing database information in relation to its existing customers. Conversely an insurance service provider that launches a deposit product, for example, cannot use data relating to existing insurance

---

3   *Tournier* v. *National Provincial and Union Bank of England* [1924] 1KB461.

customers to assess the viability of its proposed deposit product. In conclusion, only significant new developments are likely to be impacted by the second principle.

Further, the restriction will not apply to marketing activity per se. Once a customer has 'opted in' to or not 'opted out' of marketing activity, the processing of personal data to promote any new products and services is carried out under that authority. It is only in relation to processing personal data for new and different purposes where an organisation may find itself in non-compliance with the second principle. Thus in the example above of an insurance company launching a deposit product, the organisation has authority to market the product to its customers, but not to use personal data to select from its customer base for other purposes.

The restriction primarily operates where the intention is to populate one database from another including personal data. So, for example, a superstore operator that has collected personal data about its customers' buying habits via a loyalty card is prevented from using that information to assess the risk posed by its customers as, say, life insurance proposers.

The second principle also operates if the marketing consents have not been obtained correctly or are otherwise rendered invalid. In the case of the utility companies on relaxing the monopoly market for example, personal data relating to existing customers could not be used to market other services. Personal data had been obtained in a monopoly situation where consent to marketing activity was not an issue. However, the utility companies were not then allowed to approach existing customers with offers of other products and services because of the second principle. Therefore the utility companies were reduced to buying or renting mailing lists of prospects; they could not market to their own existing customers because they had no authority to do so. This was an extreme example, but nevertheless compliance with the second principle may result in the organisation having to go back to data subjects to obtain consent. If the organisation does not have authority to process personal data for specific purposes, perhaps due to inadequate subject information or changes in processing activity, consent is the only way to obtain authority to carry out the desired processing. Seeking consent from data subjects brings its own problems: time, cost and effort to carry out such a project, the risk of no reply or a negative response, and so on. It goes without saying that processing without due authority is a compliance breach and regulated organisations may find that the breach has to be reported.

RISK MANAGEMENT IN RELATION TO THE SECOND PRINCIPLE

An audit of current data processing activities will identify all the diverse purposes for which personal data is processed around the organisation. As well as principal business activities, there may be secondary processing activity, and possibly processing activities undertaken on behalf of third parties. Remember that other group companies are classified as 'third parties' for purposes of data protection law and often the regulation of financial products and services results in separate legal entities being required.

The processing of personal data for purposes related to HR management and personnel administration must also be included in any audit activity to identify all purposes for which personal data is processed in the organisation. Once all the purposes have been identified, data protection registration entries should be cross-checked to ensure that the registrations are complete and up to date. The same information can then be cross-checked against existing subject information notices. These will vary in content depending on the location of the notice and its intended audience. By identifying actual processing activity and using that information to assess where and if specified purposes match actual activity, the organisation can assess its compliance and attach a risk factor to compliance breaches and the likelihood that they will be discovered.

Forward planning is the key to continuing compliance with the second principle. Changes to the organisation's main areas of activity are likely to lead to conflicts with the second principle. A good strategy to reduce the risk of a conflict is to ensure that project teams that handle new developments, acquisitions, takeovers or mergers include a party who can advise on the data protection implications at an early stage of the project or who can obtain appropriate legal advice on the subject. If issues and potential issues are identified early in the project, solutions may be found. If the only option is to try to obtain consent, the earlier the process starts the more chance there is that a good response can be achieved before the processing begins.

Also it is important to ensure that the organisation's data protection adviser is informed of other new developments that could be outside the organisation's current registration entry and subject information notices. When planning new developments, senior managers tend to assume that access to existing customers is a given, but the first and second principles operating together may prevent access. Education of senior managers will help to establish a compliant culture.

The final piece of the jigsaw to ensure compliance with the second principle is to require any amendments to subject information statements to be signed off by the data protection compliance officer or legal adviser. One area where problems are increasingly manifest is where standard documents are not pre-printed but are held in electronic format to be printed off as required, possibly with some personalisation. There is a growing tendency to use electronic documents to replace pre-printed forms, which have to be stored at all relevant locations and destroyed when new letterhead, logo or company name is introduced. Electronic documents that allow users to edit the text are open to unauthorised amendment of key statements such as data protection notices and staff must be discouraged from making such changes or the documents themselves protected from unauthorised amendment.

LIMITED EXEMPTION – PROCESSING FOR RESEARCH PURPOSES

In limited circumstances there is an exemption from the requirement to comply with the second principle. Where processing of personal data is only undertaken for research purposes (including statistical or historical purposes), it is not to be regarded as incompatible with the purposes for which it was obtained so long as the following requirements are met:

- The data must not be processed to support measures or decisions with respect to particular individuals, although the results may be used to support future changes in relation to future prospects or customers.

- The data must not be processed in such a way that substantial damage or distress is, or is likely to be, caused to any data subject.

So, if personal data is processed for genuine research purposes, the processing need not relate to the purpose for which the data was originally obtained. However, the data must not be used to make decisions about individual data subjects. This latter rider probably negates the usefulness of the exemption for business purposes.

For example, an insurance company wants to disclose its claims records to a research foundation involved in the analysis of trends in morbidity. The insurance company is registered to process personal data for the purpose of insurance administration and it has not listed research foundations as a potential disclosure of its data. Ostensibly the disclosure of claims data to the research foundation would be in breach of the second principle, but it would be permissible under the exemption for research purposes.

Note that the insurance company would not be able to use the research or any feedback from it to identify existing claims that differed from the norm in any way. Such use would amount to making decisions about individual data subjects and would invalidate the exemption. The exemption is only operative where the processing does not support measures or decisions relating to particular individuals. The trends identified would be legitimately a factor in dealing with future claims.

CHAPTER 5

The Third Principle

Personal data shall be adequate, relevant and not excessive in relation to the purpose or purposes for which they are processed.

INTERPRETATION

The key elements in interpreting the third principle are what is meant by the words 'adequate', 'relevant', and 'excessive' respectively in the context of personal data processing. None of these terms are defined. Judgements must be made as to what is adequate, relevant and not excessive in each case and this may vary according to the circumstances.

The Information Commissioner has also provided guidance previously on the interpretation of the third principle.[1] The key issues from the Information Commissioner's perspective are:

- that this principle should be applied subjectively, that is, in relation to individual data subjects;

- that information should not be held on the basis of hitherto unidentified and undefined purposes; and

- whether or not personal data held complies with this principle will change over time and as circumstances change.

All of these areas are considered in more detail below.

PERSONAL DATA TO BE ADEQUATE FOR THE PURPOSE

Adequacy of personal data can only be judged in the light of the purpose or purposes for which it is intended it be processed. Take, for example, processing for purposes of client administration. Routine client account administration requires record-keeping in relation to transactions as well as name and contact details. The record will ordinarily include the product and/or service the client has contracted for and possibly

---

1   *The Data Protection Principles*, Guideline 4.

other products and services the client has with the organisation. All of this information, transaction record, name and contact details, details of other products provided, is required for the organisation to successfully administer the account. Any less information would be inadequate for the purposes of client account administration and some accounts will require additional information in the form of marketing preferences, complaints and compliments.

Client account administration also includes keeping records relating to former customers for a period of time so that the organisation is able to respond to requests for information from the former customer and government bodies such as the Inland Revenue or HM Revenue & Customs. Once again, certain information is required as a minimum for the closed account to be administered. If the organisation holds insufficient information to be able to meet these obligations, it will have inadequate records for the purpose for which personal data was intended to be processed.

Therefore one measure of adequacy is the ability of an organisation to meet obligations undertaken as part of the original purposes for which data was obtained and legal obligations in relation to the product or service.

Also adequacy relates not only to the information sought initially from data subjects but also to maintaining adequate records throughout the changing circumstances of the relationship. The Information Commissioner's view in relation to the retention of personal data is that the position should be reviewed and assessed at the termination of the relationship. Clearly this is a pivotal time in the development of the relationship with obvious implications for record management.

RISK MANAGEMENT

Two key areas have been identified. First, a product or service provider is under a contractual obligation to the customer to provide the product or service on the terms agreed at the outset. The organisation's record-keeping policies should be based on meeting these obligations. This is a business requirement as much as a standard for data protection compliance.

The maintenance of adequate records can be achieved and monitored through frequent reviews of forms or other methods used for collecting information about individuals. Amendment or restructuring should aim to ensure that correctly completed forms provide the right amount and type of information, or that the other methods of data collection meet this standard.

Second, the obligations of the organisation as regards meeting customer requirements and legal requirements are likely to change over time. Although a regular review should identify slight adjustments required over time, certain key events in the life of the customer relationship will help to define when independent review (independent from routine reviews) is required. A good example of this is at the termination of the relationship with the customer.

PERSONAL DATA TO BE RELEVANT TO THE PURPOSE

The relevance of personal data operates on two levels. Personal data should be relevant to the purposes for which it is to be processed and it should be relevant relative to the data subject. A good example is a particular piece of information sought on a job application form. Supposing a job application form asks whether or not the applicant holds a full UK driving licence. As a standard question on an application form, it is likely that it is not relevant because, in most cases, holding a UK driving licence will not be a requirement of the job, so it is usually not relevant to the purposes for which it is obtained, namely making a recruitment decision.

The second issue is whether or not that piece of information is relevant to the recruitment decision in a particular case. In the case of recruitment for a senior manager who will be entitled to a company car, the question is relevant, likewise it is relevant if recruitment is for a driver or a worker whose job will involve driving. Organisations are expected to differentiate between the amount and type of personal data required from a prospective senior manager to that required from someone for a more junior position.

Another example would be requesting information about an individual's savings, investments and liabilities in relation to a product sold on an execution-only basis. The barest customer details are required for an execution-only transaction, although a more thorough knowledge of the customer might be useful for marketing purposes. An organisation would not therefore be entitled to request detailed information for the purposes of selling a product on an execution-only basis; this amount of information is not relevant to an execution-only transaction.

RISK MANAGEMENT

The maintenance of relevant records relies on asking for relevant information from the data subject or others initially. It can be achieved and monitored through frequent reviews of forms used for collecting information about individuals. Amendment or restructuring should aim to ensure that correctly completed forms provide the right amount and type of information.

PERSONAL DATA NOT TO BE EXCESSIVE FOR THE PURPOSE

There is substantial overlap between what is relevant and what is not excessive. If personal data can be shown to be irrelevant, it will follow that it is excessive for the purposes for which it is processed. This was the situation in a Data Protection Tribunal case involving Runnymede Borough Council and others.[2] In this case, Community Charge Registration Officers (CCROs) from several councils were holding information about property types on the Data Protection Register. The Data Protection Registrar (now the Information Commissioner) had objected to this practice as the information was not directly relevant to the assessment of liability to community charge in most cases. The CCROs argued that the information would be available for cross-checking against future returns made by householders to identify properties that had converted from one house to several flats for example. Critically there was no standard form used by CCROs to obtain information from householders up and down the country and not all CCROs had included a reference to property type. The Tribunal noted that the information about changes to property could be elicited from other questions on the forms and therefore that the question about property type was irrelevant in many cases. Following guidance issued by the Data Protection Registrar, the Tribunal agreed that CCROs should hold the minimum of information required in each case and that, in the current instance, they had failed to identify the small proportion of cases where it might be appropriate. Therefore the only conclusion for the Tribunal was that the CCROs were holding personal data that was irrelevant and excessive in many cases.

RISK MANAGEMENT

The primary method of highlighting information that is excessive for the purpose for which it is processed is regular review, as with checks for adequacy and relevance. Both the personal data collection processes and existing records need to be checked regularly for information that is inherently excessive or because it is no longer required for the purpose. There is significant overlap with the fifth data protection principle, which relates to retention of personal data.

SUBJECTIVE JUDGMENT FOR WHAT IS ADEQUATE, RELEVANT AND NOT EXCESSIVE

The Information Commissioner will always consider how the principles apply in relation to one or more individual data subjects rather than to a database of subjects

---

2   *Runnymede Borough Council CCRO and Others* v. *The Data Protection Registrar* [1990] DA 90/24/49/3.

en masse. In guidance,[3] the Information Commissioner's Office has encouraged organisations to identify the minimum amount of information relating to each data subject that it requires to meet processing and business objectives. When judging whether personal data is adequate, relevant and not excessive for the purpose, organisations should consider the position in relation to each individual data subject as a question of fact in each case.

The Data Protection Tribunal has upheld this subjective approach in the Runnymede Borough Council case. The Tribunal also agreed with the Information Commissioner's Office's view of how the subjective test can impact on personal data processing, which is that where information is held relating to a number of individuals but is relevant only in some cases, that information is likely to be excessive for those to whom it is not relevant.

INFORMATION NOT REQUIRED FOR CURRENT OR REASONABLY IMMINENT PURPOSES

The Tribunal in the Runnymede Borough Council case did not rule out that holding certain additional information would be acceptable depending on the circumstances. It gave the example of holding details relating to residents at a property who were nearly of age to become charge payers. However, it noted that it is not relevant and would be excessive to hold wide classes of data merely on the ground that future changes in the law may in remote and uncertain future circumstances require further property types to be added to the records.

Guidance from the Information Commissioner[4] has indicated that it is not acceptable to obtain and hold information simply on the basis that it might be useful in the future, although the Information Commissioner recognises that it may be necessary to hold information in case of a particular foreseeable contingency, even though it might never occur. So, for example, it is acceptable to hold details of next of kin for term life insurance policyholders. There is no guarantee that the insured event, the death of the insured during the term of insurance, will occur but the next of kin details are a useful step to identifying executors and beneficiaries if the insured event does take place.

---

3   *The Data Protection Principles*, Guideline 4. *Legal Guidance*, para. 3.3.
4   *Legal Guidance*, section 3.3 on the third principle.

HOW ADEQUACY, RELEVANCE AND EXCESS ARE ASSESSED

Guidance on the 1984 Act[5] issued by the Information Commissioner's Office included a list of factors to be taken into account by enforcement teams when judging whether personal data was adequate, relevant and not excessive for the purpose. These are the factors:

- the number of individuals on whom data is held
- the number of individuals for whom data is used
- the nature of the item of personal data
- the length of time for which it is held
- the way it was obtained
- the possible consequences for individuals of its holding or erasure
- the way in which it is used
- the purpose for which it is held.

The point is made in the guidance that the Information Commissioner would not accept that information is relevant merely on the say so of the data controller.

THE EFFECT OF TIME ON COMPLIANCE WITH THE THIRD PRINCIPLE

Clearly the third principle applies to records kept over a period of time and covering various circumstances. At the time of obtaining personal data it must be adequate, relevant and not excessive for the purposes of, for example, providing a quote or opening an account. During the continuance of the relationship with the customer, the personal data must be adequate, relevant and not excessive for the purpose of administering the client account and communicating with the client. After the end of the relationship with the customer, personal data held in closed or archive records must be adequate, relevant and not excessive for the purpose of meeting the likely demands for information of the former customer and government bodies such as the Inland Revenue or HM Revenue & Customs. When such demands are no longer relevant, retention of the personal information would be regarded as excessive.

---

5   This is still relevant as the wording of the principle has not changed in the Data Protection Act 1998, although it was the fourth principle in the Data Protection Act 1984.

PUBLISHED GUIDANCE – SOME EXAMPLES

The following cases reported by the Information Commissioner illustrate the application of the third principle:[6]

- In processing a mortgage customer's application for a current account, a bank was found to have acted in breach of the third data protection principle when it carried out three credit reference checks on the applicant. This processing was held to be inadequate and excessive; one check should have sufficed. Also by a series of unfortunate circumstances the customer was made the subject of a marker indicating possible fraud on his bank account. The repeated credit reference checks had raised unfounded suspicions, thus having a potentially significant effect on the data subject.

- An indicator on an individual's credit reference file showed that the bank account holder had got into financial difficulties. Although this was accurate, the personal data was inadequate because the individual had entered into an agreed arrangement with the bank to rectify the situation but this had not been recorded.

- An application for a bank current account was rejected, although the applicant had a mortgage with the bank. The bank had failed to update its records to show the applicant's new address and credit reference checks were carried out on the incorrect address. As more than one credit reference check was undertaken, an automatic fraud detection programme picked up the anomaly and a marker indicating possible fraud was attached to the applicant's account. As the applicant worked in the financial services sector, it was possible that the marker could prevent him obtaining employment. An assessment was made by the Information Commissioner's Office and the finding was that this processing breached the first, third and fourth data protection principles. A review of all the relevant procedures, plus additional data protection training for staff at branch level was required.

---

6 Taken from the Information Commissioner's case histories and enquiries for 2000–2001, www.informationcommissioner.gov.uk/cms/DocumentUploads/mediasummary.doc.

CHAPTER 6

The Fourth Principle

Personal data shall be accurate and, where necessary, kept up to date.

The text of the fourth data protection principle is unchanged from the 1984 Data Protection Act, although the numbering is different; it was formerly the fifth data protection principle. The interpretation of the Principle has changed subtly. A useful proviso has been added to give some flexibility in certain cases where inaccurate data is processed despite the data controller having taken reasonable steps to ensure its accuracy.

ACCURACY

The requirement that personal data be accurate is not absolute. Where personal data is inaccurate, but the data controller can show that the information in the data is reproduced in its records exactly as it was obtained, then there is no breach of this principle. So, for example, if an insurance proposal is completed using inaccurate information that the broker or insurance company believes to be true, then neither the broker nor the insurance company is in breach of the fourth principle even though its personal data records include inaccurate information. Similarly if information is inaccurately recorded in the broker's office and passed on to the insurance company, the latter is not in breach of the principle, although its records are inaccurate. However, there is a duty on all organisations to take reasonable steps to ensure the accuracy of personal data.

Where possible, the data controller should use automated means to verify personal data, for example computer systems should be programmed so that the current year is not accepted in a date of birth data entry field. Postal code and telephone number data entry fields can be automatically restricted to a limited number of digits to assist in maintaining accuracy when recording personal data. Generally a data controller would be expected to use common sense when obtaining personal data and if it appears that information may be inaccurate, to investigate further and not accept such information at face value.

A further qualification to the requirement that personal data be accurate applies where the data controller holds information that is known or believed to be inaccurate but a note has been made on the record that this is the case. There may be occasions when retaining an original inaccuracy has value for the data controller. The fourth principle does not require an organisation to amend its records and erase the inaccurate information where it is preferable that it be retained. So, for example, a discrepancy in information supplied on a credit application form might be explained by the data subject but the data controller would wish to retain the data in its original form with an explanation of the inaccuracy. The record might be retained in this form simply as an anomaly to bear in mind in future dealings with the data subject.

PUBLISHED GUIDANCE

Guidance on the text of the fourth principle issued under the 1984 Act is still relevant, the text of the principle having remained unchanged. In *Legal Guidance*, Part 4, published in November 1994 in relation to the 1984 Act, the Registrar commented that the first part of this principle (then the fifth principle) is stated in unqualified terms; data is either accurate or it is not. However, when considering whether or not it would be appropriate to take action against a data controller found to be in breach of the part of the principle requiring accuracy, the following factors would be taken into account:

- The significance of the inaccuracy. Has it caused or is it likely to cause damage or distress to the data subject?

- The source from which the inaccurate information was obtained. Was it reasonable for the data controller to rely on information received from that source?

- Any steps taken to verify the information. Did the data controller attempt to check its accuracy with another source? Would it have been reasonable to ask the data subject, either at the time of collection or at another convenient opportunity, whether the information was accurate?

- The procedures for data entry and for ensuring that the system itself does not introduce inaccuracies into the data.

- The procedures followed by the data controller when the inaccuracy came to light. Was the data corrected as soon as the inaccuracy became apparent? Was the correction passed on to any third parties to whom the inaccurate data may already have been disclosed? Did the inaccuracy have any other consequences in the period before it was corrected? If so, what has the data controller done about those consequences?

KEEPING PERSONAL DATA UP TO DATE

The fourth principle provides that personal data must be kept up to date only where it is necessary for the purposes for which it is held. A record intended to provide a snapshot of circumstances as at a given date obviously does not need to be updated. For example, an organisation requires customers and clients to keep it advised of changes in their circumstances, such as change of address and change of name. However, it is not necessary for the organisation to update individual application forms to show the new address. The client record should show the correct address; other documentation or records might show personal data correct as at the date of opening an account, subsequent changes in details being recorded elsewhere.

PUBLISHED GUIDANCE

The Information Commissioner has stated[1] that it may be important for the purpose of the data processing that personal data be current, for example, where personal data is processed to determine whether or not to provide credit. This is an area where a data subject could suffer damage (by not being offered credit) if personal data is inaccurate. Suggested factors set out in the *Legal Guidance*[2] for data controllers to take into account are:

- any record of when personal data was obtained or updated

- awareness of the data controller that personal data may not be up to date

- any procedures to update personal data and the effectiveness of those procedures

- whether or not the non-currency of the personal data is likely to cause damage or distress to the data subject.

EXAMPLES INVOLVING THE FOURTH PRINCIPLE

Inaccurate personal data may cause damage or distress to a data subject. The following examples[3] illustrate circumstances in which it is important for personal data to be accurate and kept up to date.

- A complaint was received about personal data recorded on a credit reference file. Although the account had been written off some years earlier and the balance on the account was zero, nevertheless the impression was given that

---

1 December 2001 Legal Guidance paragraph 3.4.
2 *Legal Guidance*, para. 3.4.
3 Taken from the Information Commissioner's case histories and enquiries for 2000–2001, www.informationcommissioner.gov.uk/cms/DocumentUploads/mediasummary.doc.

the account was current. Under normal procedures an account written off would have been removed from current files after a set period, usually six years from the relevant date. With its current indicator, this particular account would remain on file indefinitely in contravention of the lender's normal practices. This was found to be a breach of the fourth principle.

- Again, the potentially significant impact on a data subject of inaccurate personal data is shown by a case involving a loan applicant. When recording details of the application incorrectly a bank operator accepted archive details automatically brought up by the computer system relating to the applicant's home address and employment. The archive details were no longer current but the operator omitted to check their currency with the loan applicant or against information provided by the loan applicant. When the bank tried to contact the applicant using the inaccurate details, it appeared as though a false address and false employment details had been provided. The bank concluded that an attempt was being made to obtain a loan fraudulently. As a result a fraud warning indicator was attached to the file and may have been shared with other financial institutions in due course. The potential for damage to the data subject is clear as well as it being a breach of the fourth principle.

- Inaccurate personal data can give a misleading impression. Two individuals who had been married and were now divorced complained that a credit reference agency had failed to note that the two were not connected. The root of the problem was an incorrect assumption by a member of the agency's staff that the two were in fact still financially connected. This was found to be a breach of the fourth principle.

- Another breach of the fourth principle involved a police force that mistakenly attributed another person's record to an individual undergoing an employment vetting check. The individual complained that this constituted a breach of the Data Protection Act. The police force agreed to modify its procedures to prevent a recurrence and made an ex-gratia payment to the individual.

- Organisations that record images of street activity for crime prevention purposes should not need to retain images for longer than 31 days unless they are required for evidential purposes in legal proceedings.

- Banks and building societies recording images at ATMs for the purposes of resolving customer disputes might reasonably retain recorded images for up to three months in order to provide information about cash withdrawals. The Information Commissioner suggests this retention period based on the intervals at which individuals receive their account statements.

PERMANENT DELETION OF DATA HELD ON COMPUTER

There is an additional compliance problem with deleting data from computer systems in order to comply with the fifth principle. The Information Commissioner is aware that computer systems do not always lend themselves to permanently deleting data or to anonymising personal data.[5] The guidance suggests that the organisation take such technical and organisational measures as are necessary to ensure that anonymised information cannot be reconstituted to become personal information and that they should also be prepared to justify any decision they make in relation to processing such data.

PURGING FILES AND RECORDS

The fifth principle is a clear instruction to purge unwanted personal data from records and documents. Most organisations implement purging by adopting a document and file retention policy. There are two problems with document retention policies. First, the policies refer to documents rather than the personal data they contain. The fifth principle refers to 'personal data' rather than documents, so there is an initial mismatch. Another issue here is that personal data is held in files together with other information that is not personal data. In many cases, personal data will permeate a file of documents and, depending on the nature of the personal data, it may have different retention periods. The fifth principle intrinsically requires the purging of files as well as file destruction because it relates to personal data, not to actual files that include personal data. The only way to extract personal data from a file is to purge it. Many organisations do not have a culture where purging files is encouraged or required. Generally, files are archived pending final destruction. No one takes the time to extract unnecessary personal data before archiving the file. The decision in the Durant case and the precedent it set in relation to the definition of a 'relevant filing system' has eased this problem to some extent.

---

5   *Legal Guidance*, para. 2.2.5.

The lack of purging activity is a compliance problem. It is highly likely that archived files contain personal data that is no longer required and that should be deleted or destroyed to meet the requirements of the fifth principle.

The Durant decision applies the definition of a relevant filing system (that is, one within the scope of data protection law) narrowly; paper files form part of a relevant filing system only if they are in a system that provides the same or similar accessibility as a computer filing system. Therefore, the filing system must both appear to be one which provides easy accessibility either by indexation or clear labelling, and allow the identification at the outset of whether a file or set of files within the system contains information relating to a specific data subject. Therefore an archive filing system may not fall within the definition of a relevant filing system. Archive files tend to be more loosely indexed and referenced than those in current use.

Second, data retention policies refer to retaining files and information; they rarely specify what should be done with documents and data once the specified retention periods have expired. The implication of the fifth principle is that documents containing personal data and information comprising personal data should be destroyed and deleted respectively once they are no longer required for the purpose for which they are held. In practice, many organisations find it difficult to order the destruction of files. There may be a nagging doubt as to whether or not the information may still be required. There is another problem when personal data is held on computer as many systems do not allow data to be deleted permanently. Even though an individual user may 'delete' data, it is often recoverable in IT terms.

An example of the dual obligations of the fifth principle, to purge and to destroy files, is given in the *Employment Practices Data Protection Code*. This recommends that employers establish appropriate employee record retention policies based on the business need and that these should be rigorously adhered to.[6] One of the early drafts of the *Employment Practices Data Protection Code* included a suggested table of retention periods relating to HR files and records.

The table itemises the routine contents of a personnel file. An appropriate retention period is suggested for each category of record, which varies according to the perceived need to meet business needs and legal and regulatory requirements. Note also that it is suggested that a summary be retained for a longer period than the full records. The summary would have to be produced from the full records as a specific task.

Both of the activities impliedly required to comply with the fifth principle cause problems for organisations. Purging the contents of a file or record rather than simply

---

6   Information Commissioner (2005) Part 1 'Recruitment and Selection', benchmark 8.1, *The Employment Practices Data Protection Code*. Available from www.informationcommissioner.gov.uk.

archiving it en masse, and creating summaries of key records are both time-consuming activities for which modern office administration does not cater.

Document	Suggested period of retention	Keep or delete on employee leaving
Application form	Duration of employment	Delete/destroy
References	1 year	Delete/destroy
Payroll and tax information	6 years	Keep 6 years
Sickness records	3 years	Delete/destroy
Annual leave records	2 years	Delete/destroy
Unpaid leave/special leave records	3 years	Delete/destroy
Annual appraisal/assessment records	5 years	Delete/destroy
Records relating to promotion, transfer, training, disciplinary matters	1 year from end of employment	Keep 1 year
References given/information supporting the reference	5 years from giving reference	Keep 5 years from giving reference
Summary of record of service such as name, position held, dates of employment	10 years from end of employment	Keep 10 years
Records relating to accident or injury at work	12 years	Keep 12 years

EXEMPTION FOR DATA HELD FOR RESEARCH PURPOSES

Records that are retained for purposes of research should have personal data removed where possible, anonymising the records so that no data subjects are identifiable from the information retained.

Section 33 of the Data Protection Act (1998) provides that personal data held only for research purposes (including statistical or historical purposes) may be held indefinitely (as an exception to the provisions of the fifth principle) so long as the following requirements are met:

● The data must not be processed to support measures or decisions with respect to the particular data subjects whose details are processed.

● The data must not be processed in such a way that substantial damage or distress is, or is likely to be, caused to any data subject.

This useful exemption under section 33 is not lost even where:

● personal data is disclosed to another person so long as it is for research purposes only;

● it is disclosed to the data subject, at his request or with his consent;

● it is disclosed to a person acting on behalf of the data subject;

● a person makes the disclosure reasonably believing that the disclosure falls with these grounds when in fact it does not.

COMPLIANCE STRATEGIES

Part of the compliance procedure for processing personal data in accordance with the fifth principle is to ensure that appropriate document retention policies and guidelines are in place and followed. In addition, if the organisation's stated retention periods for personal data differ from what would normally be expected to apply, the reasons for an unusual retention period or unusual deletion policy should be documented for future reference. Organisations should ensure that as well as specifying document retention periods, policies also refer to what should happen to files and documents when the retention period expires.

Compliance with the fifth principle involves purging files and records and sometimes creating summaries, both activities involving time that modern office administration does not usually allow for. Management should be aware that failure to manage files and records as suggested is a compliance risk. Consideration should be given to introducing administrative personnel dedicating to implementing purge and deletion policies. As long as clear guidelines and a process for escalating queries are provided, a junior member of staff should be able to carry out the role.

There is no compliance solution to the issue of permanent computer records or those records that have been 'anonymised' but where the original personal data is still held and could, theoretically at least, be reconstituted as personal data. Management should be aware of these types of issues so that it can make decisions on a managed risk basis.

CHAPTER 8

The Sixth Principle

Personal data shall be processed in accordance with the rights of data subjects under this Act.

Subject rights are set out in Part II of the Data Protection Act 1998 (the Act), sections 7 to 15. Since October 2001 all the subject rights have been in force, although subject access to certain limited paper files can still benefit from the exemption provided by the second transitional period. As this exemption is restricted to information held on paper subject to processing already underway as at 24 October 1998 and to personal data processed for certain historical research purposes only, it is not dealt with in this book.

The principles are set out in Schedule 1 to the Data Protection Act 1998. Part II of Schedule 1 contains provisions to assist with the interpretation of the principles. In relation to the sixth principle, Part II of Schedule 1 lists the data subject rights that have the benefit of the principle. It is important to note that the sixth principle does not establish an open-ended obligation to process personal data in accordance with rights as yet undefined. By listing the data subject rights to which the sixth principle applies, Part II defines the extent of its application. It applies to:

- section 7, the right of access to personal data by the data subject (known as a 'subject access request');

- section 10, notice from a data subject that they are exercising their right to prevent processing likely to cause damage or distress to themselves or another;

- section 11, notice from a data subject that personal data relating to them should not continue to be processed for purposes of direct marketing;

- section 12, notice requiring the data controller to ensure that certain decisions taken by automated means be reviewed.

Other data subject rights are created by the Data Protection Act 1998 (the Act) but these are rights granted on application to the Court, and they do not have the protection of the sixth principle. These are:

- The right to compensation for breaches of the Act in certain circumstances.

- Rights in relation to inaccurate data.

There are yet other rights, created by the Sensitive Data Order 2000.[1] The order sets out conditions for fair processing of sensitive data which supplement those set out in Schedule 3 to the Act. Certain of these conditions are qualified by allowing data subjects the right to prevent processing of sensitive data relating to them under the condition.

The individual subject rights are considered below.

SUBJECT ACCESS REQUEST

Data subjects have a right to a copy of any information comprising personal data relating to them that is in the control of the data controller. 'Control' means in the data controller's possession or in the possession of a party over which the data controller has power to demand its possession. This is the case, for example, where personal data is in the possession of a data processor that processes the data on behalf of the data controller.

Note also that the data subject has the right to a copy of the information comprising personal data, not a copy of every document that features personal data. So although it may generally be quicker and easier to copy an entire file that relates to a data subject on request, it may be that the only personal data contained in a file of correspondence is the name and address of the data subject as the addressee. In these circumstances it is permissible to provide simply the name and address as information comprising personal data in the possession of the data controller.

A data subject who makes a request under section 7 for a copy of their personal data is entitled to:

- confirmation that the organisation holds personal data relating to them;
- be advised of the purposes for which personal data relating to them is processed; and
- be advised of the sources of the personal data.

In addition, on request a data subject is entitled to:

- be advised if the data is subject to any automated decision-making process; and

---

1   The Data Protection (Processing of Sensitive Data) Order 2000 (417).

- be advised of the logic involved in any automated processing in certain circumstances.

These obligations go much further than the original right of access under the Data Protection Act 1984. Disclosure of the logic involved in any automated processing might cause problems, in particular for organisations that use automated underwriting to assess insurance or credit risks. Such disclosure could facilitate selection against the organisation, as knowledge of the selection criteria would allow answers to questions to be manipulated to give the desired outcome.

The use of systems involving an automated decision-making process relates to another right under the Act. Section 12 allows an individual to object to a decision made by automated means in certain circumstances. The disclosure that decisions are being made by automated means as a requirement of meeting a subject access request under section 7 facilitates the exercise of the section 12 right. However, the data controller does not have to comply with this part of the subject access request if the disclosure of the logic involved in the automated processing would constitute the disclosure of a 'trade secret'.

The issue for the organisation is whether or not the disclosure of information would assist an enquirer in perpetrating a fraud such as manipulating responses to credit scoring or underwriting questions to select against the organisation. The issue from the perspective of the regulator is whether that is the same as a trade secret. Consider, though, that just because non-disclosure is in the best interests of the data controller it does not necessarily follow that it is a trade secret.

Data controllers may charge data subjects a fee of up to £10 to help towards administration costs. The data controller has 40 days from receipt of the fee in which to consider the validity of the request, whether any exemptions apply and to supply the information requested or explain why certain information is being withheld.

An explanation of codes and references used in the information must be provided if the meaning is not clear. The information must be provided in legible, permanent form unless an alternative medium is agreed with the data subject or if providing it in permanent form would involve disproportionate effort. The term 'disproportionate effort' is not defined but is a matter of fact in each case. Guidance from the Information Commissioner suggests that factors such as the cost of providing the information, the length of time likely to be taken to produce the information and how difficult it may be for the data controller to provide it should be balanced against the rights of the individual in each case. Disproportionate effort was quoted in an example involving a request for access to CCTV images showing an incident where a door came off its hinges near to a family walking in a shopping mall. The circumstances were that the CCTV system recorded images with 3-second delays between frames. One frame showed the door in place, the subsequent frame showed the door laid on the floor near the family of shoppers. A family member had requested a copy of the footage but as the footage did not show the actual event, was expensive and time consuming to copy and the organisation had already admitted liability, the request was turned down on grounds of disproportionate effort.

There are limited exceptions to the requirement to comply fully with a valid subject access request.[2] For the most part, the exceptions apply in relation to specific information that may be withheld from the data subject on specific grounds. Only if the data subject fails to comply with the formalities of making a subject access request, does the Act allow the data controller to decline to supply personal data when in receipt of a subject access request.

The list of exceptions that follows is not comprehensive but considers some of those more generally applicable.

EXCEPTION WHERE THE FORMALITIES HAVE NOT BEEN COMPLIED WITH

A data controller is not obliged to comply with a request for subject access unless they have received:

- a request in writing; and

- a fee not exceeding £10 if applicable (a lower fee applies to credit reference agencies and a higher one to certain health records); and

- such information as they may reasonably require in order to satisfy themselves as to the identity of the person making the request and to locate the information sought.

The Freedom of Information Act 2000 has added a further proviso to the final point.[3] Where a data controller reasonably requires further information to confirm the identity of the data subject and to locate the information sought, they may ask the data subject for more information. If that further information is not supplied, the data controller is not under a duty to comply with the subject access request.

---

2   Set out in the Data Protection Act 1998, Schedule 7, section 7 and various orders made under the Act.
3   The Freedom of Information Act 2000, section 7(3).

EXCEPTION FOR PERSONAL DATA RELATING TO OTHER DATA SUBJECTS ('THIRD PARTIES')

Where compliance with a subject access request would necessarily involve the disclosure of information relating to another individual (including the fact that information has been provided by that third party) who can be identified from that information, the data controller is not obliged to provide information relating to the third party unless:

- the third party has consented to the disclosure of the information to the person making the request; or

- it is reasonable in all the circumstances to comply with the request without the consent of the third party.

In this context what is 'reasonable' depends on:

- any duty of confidentiality owed to the third party;

- any steps taken by the data controller to obtain the consent of the third party;

- whether the third party is capable of giving or refusing consent.

Note that this exemption only applies to information that relates to a third party; other information comprising personal data should still be disclosed to the data subject in response to a subject access request.

Published guidance

Guidance has been published by the Information Commissioner[4] about how to deal with subject access requests that will result in personal data relating to a third party being disclosed. In particular, advising the enquirer the source of personal data relating to them will often result in disclosing another person's personal data. The Information Commissioner identifies key questions for data controllers when dealing with subject access requests involving the potential disclosure of personal data relating to third parties:

- Does the information being accessed contain information about a third party?

- If so, would its disclosure reveal the identity of the third party?

---

4 Information Commission (2000) *Subject Access Rights and Third Party Information.* London: Data Protection Registrar; *Legal Guidance* para. 4.1.4.

- In deciding this, has other information which the data subject has, or may receive, been taken into account?

- To what extent can the information be edited so it can be supplied without revealing the identify of the third party?

- Has the third party previously given the information to the person making the subject access request?

- If, or to the extent that, the information will identify the third party, has the third party consented to the disclosure?

- If not, should consent be sought?

- Is it reasonable to disclose the third-party information without consent?

- Is the third-party information confidential or sensitive or harmful?

- Is the third-party information of particular importance to the person making the subject access request?

There is a key exception to the third-party rules suggested above. If the subject access request relates to health records and the third party is a health professional who has compiled or contributed to the health record (or has been involved in the care of the data subject in their capacity as a health professional) then access cannot be refused on the grounds that the identity of a third party would be disclosed. There is a specific exemption from the disclosure of health records in response to a subject access request (see below).

EXCEPTION RELATING TO CREDIT REFERENCE AGENCIES

Unless the data subject requests full information from a credit reference agency, the credit reference agency is entitled to assume that a subject access request relates only to the information about the subject's financial standing.

EXCEPTION RELATING TO HEALTH RECORDS

This exemption applies where a health professional considers that serious harm is likely to be caused to the data subject's physical or mental health or condition by allowing access to personal data.[5]

Before deciding whether this exemption applies, any data controller who is not a health professional is obliged to consult the health professional responsible for the clinical care of the data subject (the 'appropriate' health professional – there are provisions for where there is more than one such health professional or none at all).

---

5   Data Protection (Subject Access Modification) (Health) Order 2000.

The obligation to consult does not apply where the data subject has already seen or knows about the information that is the subject of the request, nor in certain limited circumstances where consultation has been carried out prior to the request being made.

There are provisions applying where a request is made by a third party on behalf of the data subject, which apply if the data subject is a minor or mentally incapacitated.

A health record is defined in the Act as being any record that consists of information relating to the physical or mental health or condition of an individual, and has been made by, or on behalf of, a health professional in connection with the care of that individual.

A 'health professional' is any of the following:

- *a registered medical practitioner (a 'registered medical practitioner' includes any person who is provisionally registered under section 15 or 21 of the Medical Act 1983 and is engaged in such employment as is mentioned in subsection (3) of that section);*

- *a registered dentist as defined by section 53(1) of the Dentists Act 1984;*

- *a registered optician as defined by section 36(1) of the Opticians Act 1989;*

- *a registered pharmaceutical chemist as defined by section 24(1) of the Pharmacy Act 1954 or a registered person as defined by Article 2(2) of the Pharmacy (Northern Ireland) Order 1976;*

- *a registered nurse, midwife or health visitor;*

- *a registered osteopath as defined by section 41 of the Osteopaths Act 1993;*

- *a registered chiropractor as defined by section 43 of the Chiropractors Act 1994;*

- *any person who is registered as a member of a profession to which the Professions Supplementary to Medicine Act 1960 for the time being extends;*

- *a clinical psychologist, child psychotherapist or speech therapist;*

- *a music therapist employed by a health service body, and*

- *a scientist employed by such a body as head of department.*

EXCEPTION RELATING TO CERTAIN REFERENCES

There is a limited exception for references in the hands of the referee. Personal data are exempt from a subject access request if they consist of a reference given, or to be given, in confidence by the data controller for the purposes of education, training or employment.

Note that the exemption does not apply in the hands of the recipient of the reference, therefore it is of limited use. Once the reference has been received by the organisation requesting it, this exemption is lost. If the subject of the reference makes a subject access request to the recipient organisation, it must then consider the exception from the need to comply where personal data relating to a third party, in this case the referee, would be disclosed. As noted above, this is an area where the data controller has to make a judgement on the balance of rights of the individuals concerned. A key circumstance would be whether or not the reference was supplied subject to any duty of confidentiality. However, given the potentially significant impact of an unfavourable reference on the life and livelihood of a data subject, particularly in a regulated industry, it would seem that the rights of the data subject are likely to outweigh the rights of the referee even where a reference was taken up in confidence.

EXCEPTION FOR MANAGEMENT FORECASTS

Personal data processed for the purposes of management forecasting or management planning to assist the data controller in the conduct of any business or other activity are exempt from subject access. The exemption applies only to the extent to which subject access would be likely to prejudice the conduct of the business. This includes circumstances, for example, where relocation of the business or part of it is under consideration and specific individuals are being considered either for relocation with the business or for redundancy. A subject access request from a data subject in these circumstances could be handled without providing access to the planning and discussion relating to the business relocation if that would prejudice the relocation. Note that the key issue is to avoid prejudice to the planned activity, not to avoid embarrassment to the organisation or its directors by making a decision known prior to the planned publication date.

CORPORATE FINANCE EXEMPTION

This exemption applies when responding to a subject access request could reveal price-sensitive business information. Obviously it will only apply to, and in relation to, companies whose shares are traded on a recognised stock market.

Businesses involved in providing a corporate finance service, offering underwriting or advice on issues of shares and other instruments, are exempt from responding to certain subject access requests. The exemption also applies to businesses generally to restrict access to price-sensitive information so that the orderly functioning of financial markets is not prejudiced.[6]

EXCEPTION FOR NEGOTIATIONS WITH THE DATA SUBJECT

If negotiations are underway between the data controller and the data subject, this exemption may apply to prevent the data subject from accessing details of the data controller's intentions towards them. Otherwise, the subject access provisions would operate to force the data controller to show their hand.

The exemption only applies to the extent that disclosure to meet subject information requirements would be likely to prejudice those negotiations. So, personal data which consist of records of the intentions of the data controller in relation to any negotiations with the data subject are exempt from the subject information provisions.

EXCEPTION FOR PERSONAL DATA SUBJECT TO LEGAL PROFESSIONAL PRIVILEGE

Personal data are exempt from subject access if the data consist of information in respect of which a claim to legal professional privilege could be maintained in legal proceedings. This is restrictive in real terms. Legal professional privilege is not very wide; it only applies to advice from a legal adviser to the data controller.

EXCEPTION ON GROUNDS OF SELF-INCRIMINATION

A person need not comply with any request or order regarding subject access to the extent that it would reveal evidence of criminal activity by the data controller. Disclosure to meet a subject access request should not involve the data controller in revealing the commission of any offence (other than an offence under the Act) or expose them to proceedings for that offence.

OTHER DATA SUBJECT RIGHTS

THE RIGHT TO PREVENT PROCESSING LIKELY TO CAUSE DAMAGE OR DISTRESS

Section 10 of the Act gives a right to data subjects to prevent processing likely to cause damage or distress. The Act requires that data subjects give notice to the data controller, in writing, setting out the reasons why processing is causing or is likely to

---

6   Data Protection (Corporate Finance Exemption) Order 2000 (184).

cause substantial damage or distress to themselves or another and that the damage or distress is or would be unwarranted.

The data controller then has a period of 21 days in which to respond either that they have complied or intend to comply with the request, or giving reasons for not complying. A response to the effect that the data controller does not intend to comply wholly or in part with the request must make out a case that the request is unjustified and state the grounds for that opinion. The data subject may apply to the court for a decision as to whether or not the continued processing, and the data controller's decision, is justified in the circumstances.

Exceptions to this right are set out in paragraphs 1 to 4 of Schedule 2 to the Act. They are:

- where the data subject has given consent to the processing;

- where processing is necessary for the performance of a contract to which the data subject is a party or for taking steps preliminary to entering into such a contract;

- where processing is necessary for compliance with any legal obligation to which the data controller is subject, other than a contractual obligation; and

- where processing is necessary in order to protect the vital interests of the data subject.

In an unreported court case on this point, a photograph of a disabled child playing at a creche facility was used years later by a local authority as part of a campaign to highlight the dangers of AIDS. The inference was that the child had AIDS, which was not the case. The parents of the child initially wrote to the local authority running the campaign to ask that the use of their child's picture in the campaign cease, the local authority ignored their appeal and reran the campaign. Although the case was clear cut – the local authority had behaved very poorly – damages awarded were minimal, which may deter cases being brought in future, undermining the effectiveness of the Act.

The Information Commissioner at the time of writing (2005), Richard Thomas, has suggested that a breach whose root is of a systemic nature might be dealt with in such a way that the fines are multiplied by a reasonable estimate of the number of records affected. This would certainly give more substantial encouragement to organisations to ensure that their systems are compliant. In one recent case, an accountant was found guilty under section 55 of unlawful obtaining and or disclosure of personal information. The accountant had been an agent for Bradford & Bingley building society and as such had introduced a number of clients to the building society. When the building society terminated its agency agreement with the accountant, he contacted clients and advised them to close their building society accounts and open new ones with a bank where he had a new agency agreement in place. As the defendant asked for a significant number of offences to be taken into account, the fine levied by the court was £10 000.

RIGHT TO PREVENT PROCESSING FOR THE PURPOSES OF DIRECT MARKETING

Section 11 of the Act gives data subjects the right to prevent processing of personal data relating to them for the purposes of direct marketing. A data subject may make a written request at any time to ask the data controller to cease, or not to begin, processing their personal data for the purposes of direct marketing. 'Direct marketing' means the communication (by whatever means) of any advertising or marketing material that is directed at specified individuals. Therefore mailshots, emails and telephone calls are all included.

The Act requires that such requests be made in writing and gives the data controller a 'reasonable' period in which to amend records and prospect databases to comply with the request.

RIGHT TO OBJECT TO DECISIONS TAKEN BY AUTOMATED MEANS

Under section 12 of the Act, a data subject has the right to object to decisions taken by automated means in circumstances where the decision:

- is taken by or on behalf of the organisation; and
- significantly affects that individual; and
- is based solely on the processing by automatic means of the individual's personal data; and
- is a decision taken for the purpose of evaluating matters relating to them.

The requirement is for the objection to be set out in writing. Examples of areas likely to be affected are:

- automated recruitment systems
- automated marking of psychometric and other tests
- credit scoring
- underwriting.

The data controller is under a legal obligation to review the decision taken by automated means. The reviewer must be a human being. The reviewer may concur or disagree with the automated decision.

RIGHTS NOT COVERED BY THE SIXTH PRINCIPLE

This section deals with other rights under the Act, which are not subject to the sixth principle. These rights are granted on application to the Court, and they do not have the protection of the sixth principle. They are:

- the right to compensation for breaches of the Act in certain circumstances
- rights in relation to inaccurate data
- rights created by the Sensitive Data Order 2000.

RIGHT TO COMPENSATION

Any individual who suffers harm by reason of contravention of any of the requirements of the Act is entitled to compensation from the data controller pursuant to section 13 of the Act. Similarly the individual is entitled to compensation if he suffers distress as well as damage or for distress only if the contravention relates to processing of personal data for special purposes.

'Special purposes' means one or more of the following:

- the purposes of journalism
- artistic purposes
- literary purposes.

Actual financial loss was recoverable under the 1984 Act if it was due to actions in contravention of the Act. The 1998 Act has extended the right to include compensation for damage or distress due to contravention of the Act.

RIGHTS IN RELATION TO INACCURATE DATA

A data subject may apply to the Court for rectification, blocking, erasure or destruction of personal data relating to them on the basis that the data is inaccurate pursuant to section 14 of the Act. This applies even when the data controller obtained the inaccurate data from a third party or the data subject. The Court may also choose to require the data controller's records (and the records of any other data controllers holding the same data) to be supplemented with data recording the true facts as approved by the Court.

Compensation may also be awarded by the Court if the data subject has suffered damage as a result of the inaccurate data.

RIGHT TO PREVENT PROCESSING OF SENSITIVE DATA

A feature of the Sensitive Data Order 2000 is that it gives data subjects the right to require a data controller to cease processing sensitive data relating to them if the processing is undertaken for the purposes of identifying and monitoring equal opportunities in relation to religious beliefs, physical or mental health or political views.

Exercise of the right must be by notice in writing to the data controller. A reasonable period must be stated at the end of which the data controller is required to have ceased processing. The data controller must have ceased processing those personal data at the end of that period.

RISK MANAGEMENT STRATEGIES

The risk here is that either a request or notice purporting to exercise a subject right is not identified or that it is dealt with in a non-compliant way. There are time limits to respect when responding to subject rights that any delay in identifying the purpose of a request may reduce still further. To guard against the failure to identify correctly when a subject right is being exercised, data protection rights training for staff likely to receive such requests, or come into contact with data subjects, is essential.

Good procedures are key to compliant handling of subject rights with particular emphasis on the applicable time limits, so that all those involved in the procedure on behalf of the organisation are aware of the limits. Standard form letters can help to save time and allow the organisation to take care over the way it is presented as dealing with subject rights.

Subject rights apply equally to employees as to clients and customers. Procedures should be modified to apply to staff requests; for example, it may not be desirable to charge a fee for staff who ask to see their personnel file.

CHAPTER 9

The Seventh Principle

Appropriate technical and organisational measures shall be taken against unauthorised or unlawful processing of personal data and against accidental loss or destruction of, or damage to, personal data.

The seventh principle is concerned primarily with the security of personal data. The basic requirement is that appropriate security must be in place to protect personal data from loss, damage or disclosure, whether accidental or as a result of unlawful processing. The more sensitive or confidential the information and the more harm that would result from accidental loss or disclosure of it, the tighter the security required.

In addition to the basic requirement that personal data be held securely, there are two additional requirements. The first relates to staff whose job involves handling personal data. Employers are under a legal duty to ensure that such staff are reliable. The second relates to outsourcing. Data controllers are under a legal duty to ensure that their data processors take appropriate security measures throughout the life of their relationship. Further, data controllers are responsible for putting a written contract in place with their data processors including two specific clauses relating to the seventh principle.

BASIC REQUIREMENT FOR SECURITY OF PERSONAL DATA

The requirement in the Data Protection Act 1998 (the Act) is for appropriate security of personal data. Guidance about determining what might be 'appropriate' is provided in the interpretive provisions and provides that organisations should consider the following:

- *Having regard to the state of technological development and the cost of implementing any measures, the measures must ensure a level of security appropriate to –*

  - *the harm that might result from such unauthorised or unlawful processing or accidental loss, destruction or damage as are mentioned in the seventh principle, and*

  - *the nature of the data to be protected.*[1]

---

1   The text of the Data Protection Act 1998, Schedule 1, Part II, para. 9. Author's phrasing and use of bullet points.

The interpretive provisions explain that this is not an absolute obligation and spell out the factors to take into account when assessing the appropriateness of security measures.

The first point is that the appropriateness of security measures will be assessed by reference to the state of technological development. Organisations should keep abreast of developments in record-keeping systems, particularly in their own industry. The standard of security systems prevalent in the industry sector is likely to be the benchmark for other organisations of a similar size in the sector.

Second, the cost of security measures is expressly to be factored into the assessment of what is appropriate. It would seem that 'appropriateness' in relation to cost will be influenced by the financial standing of the data controller. Costs that would be appropriate if borne by a big corporate such as BP or Shell Oil might not be appropriate if the data controller is a small business.

The nature of the data to be protected dictates, to some extent, the harm that might result from unauthorised access, unauthorised processing, loss or damage. (Processing includes obtaining, using, holding and destroying personal data.) A greater degree of harm is likely to ensue from the unauthorised disclosure of, say, sensitive data relating to a person's health than from the unauthorised disclosure of personal data such as an individual's name and address, which might be found in a telephone directory in any event.

Sensitive categories of data are not the only categories of personal data that might give rise to an increased duty of care when processing personal data. Financial data relating to earnings or tax status would be regarded by the individual concerned as confidential and the scope for harm to result from unauthorised disclosure is accordingly greater.

The Information Commissioner's view is that there can be no standard set of security measures to meet the requirements of the seventh principle.[2] Different security measures will be required to meet different circumstances. As the assessment of appropriateness of security measures depends partly on the perception of likely harm from unauthorised access, processing or destruction of personal data, the Information Commissioner encourages data controllers to adopt a risk-based approach to security.[3]

---

2   *Legal Guidance*, para. 3.7.
3   *Legal Guidance*, para. 3.7.

COMPLYING WITH THE SEVENTH DATA PROTECTION PRINCIPLE

The seventh principle requires both technical and organisational security measures to be taken to protect personal data.

The widespread use of laptop computers presents a physical risk to personal data because of the ease with which they can be carried off and the fact that they are often moved from one location to another. It is no longer sufficient simply to think and plan in terms of firewalls, password security and backup facilities; organisational security measures are also a necessary component of a realistic computer security programme.

The impact of the inclusion of paper files in a relevant filing system within the scope of the Act means that technical security measures alone cannot suffice to protect personal data against unlawful access, damage or destruction. Safeguarding paper files requires a different approach to that for computer file and database security.

Despite recommending a risk-based approach to security measures, the Information Commissioner expects certain fundamental business protection measures to be in place in any organisation. For computer systems these would include the following technical measures:

- firewall protection for internet connections to restrict hacking capability and protect against virus infection

- virus identification and protection software to remove or at least reduce the threat of viruses

- restricted access to databases on a 'need to know' basis to prevent unauthorised access and tampering

- password protection for computer systems to prevent unauthorised access and tampering

- backup facilities so that systems problems do not disable the organisation's access to personal data and so that damaged or lost files can be recovered.

Organisational measures should include some or all of the following:

- Building and office security;
  - CCTV to protect vulnerable areas and discourage staff and strangers from inappropriate activity;
  - burglar alarms to protect premises and discourage strangers from trying to access offices out of hours;

– visitor sign-in policies to control access to areas where personal information is stored and processed;

– locking external doors to prevent access to personal information out of office hours.

● Office working practices:

– fax security procedures so that confidential incoming documents are retrieved in a timely fashion and confidential outgoing documents are not sent unless the sender has checked that someone is there to retrieve it at the receiving fax machine;

– email security policies to remind staff that email is a medium that creates a written record and that the Internet is not ordinarily a secure transmission medium unless a padlock sign is displayed or it is a secure Internet or intranet link;

– secure archive facilities allowing for safe-keeping and easy retrieval of documents;

– confidential waste disposal arrangements for secure document and file destruction;

– clean desk policy so that personal data is not left on view or accessible in offices or branches out of office hours;

– use of screen savers and lock-out on unattended computer monitors and terminals to prevent eavesdropping;

– careful siting of computer monitors and terminals to prevent eavesdropping from outside the building;

– confidential document password protection to restrict access to confidential material;

– secure filing facilities.

In addition to the technical and organisational measures outlined above, organisations should review their data processing operations to identify particular risks to personal data. This is where a risk-based approach, recommended by the Information Commissioner, can be adopted.

The degree of risk is determined by a variety of factors including the effect of a particular compliance breach, the likelihood of it occurring, the number of people likely to be affected and the cost of preventive action. So, for example, the risk that an employee will divulge personal data for purposes not connected with the business or their job has a higher priority if the personal data concerned relates to the subject's financial position than if it were simply their name and address. However, there are circumstances when unauthorised disclosure of a name and address can have an unexpected and devastating result; for example, where a spouse is tracking down a partner who has moved in with a new partner. In this example the cost of preventive action is marginal. The only way to ensure that staff are aware of the confidential nature of the information they handle is by training. Confidentiality is a business need in any event, especially in the financial services industry. All that is required is for confidentiality awareness training to include the criminal offence under the Act[4] for individual employees who make unauthorised disclosure of personal data.

Some examples of particular actions that an organisation might take to combat specific risks are:

- home working policies including security aspects as well as supplying computer equipment for home workers to ensure that adequate firewall and virus protection is in place as well as the required functionality of the server;

- additional log-on requirements for shared computers and strict clean desk policies for shared desks where staff 'hot desk' or share jobs;

- strict procedures and regular monitoring to ensure that documents are not left on shared printers, perhaps even designating a responsible member of staff to police the printer and remove and deliver its output;

- secure intranet links between offices or branches which need to exchange personal data electronically;

- secure Internet links for customers who perform tasks or submit personal data online;

- warranties and contractual obligations for courier firms used to transfer personal data between locations – employing only reputable courier firms;

- warranties and contractual obligations for private investigator firms used to trace debtors or establish the veracity of insurance claims – employing only reputable firms and monitoring their activities.

With many of these measures problems arise if procedures are inadequate or inadequately communicated to staff. The organisation must establish appropriate procedures, train staff to follow them and then monitor to ensure that they are being observed. Issues also arise with new, contract or temporary staff. Organisations should be able to demonstrate how they communicate company policies, procedures and good working practices to new starters. There are, of course, security measures that

---

4   The Data Protection Act 1998, section 55.

relate wholly to control of employees and they are considered in the next section of this chapter.

Current problems – 'phishing'

'Phishing' involves the theft of identity via the Internet, which then allows the thief to obtain a pecuniary advantage, either emptying bank or savings accounts or obtaining credit, loans and credit cards.[5] This is a relatively new security challenge faced by institutions in the financial services sector and technology is struggling to provide a solution currently. Therefore, the security afforded personal data by financial institutions is being compromised daily. Fortunately the seventh principle requires security to be 'appropriate' and 'state of the art' so it suffices for online financial services providers to ensure that they keep pace with technological and organisational security developments, perhaps most importantly with those developments embraced by others in the sector, so as not to fall behind in comparative terms.

EMPLOYEES AND THE SECURITY OF PERSONAL DATA

The data protection principles are set out in Schedule 1 to the Act. Part I of Schedule 1 sets out the text of the principles and Part II of Schedule 1 adds interpretive provisions. The provisions in Part II that apply to the seventh principle state:[6]

> *The data controller must take reasonable steps to ensure the reliability of any employees of his who have access to the personal data.*

Employers have a duty to ensure the security of personal data of which they are the data controller by reference to controlling the activities of their employees. Note that this is not an absolute obligation; the requirement is simply that reasonable steps be taken. The requirement is also a continuing one. Controls are required both prior to the employee gaining access to personal data and on a continuing basis.

What is reasonable will, of course, depend on the circumstances but the *Employment Practices Data Protection Code* published by the Information Commissioner in stages between 2000 and 2003 (the *Employment Code*) gives some guidance on what steps an employer might reasonably be expected to take. First, employers are to ensure that staff

> *are aware of the extent to which they can be criminally liable if they knowingly or recklessly disclose personal data outside their employer's policies and procedures.*[7]

---

5   For further details of 'phishing', see Chapter 17.
6   The Data Protection Act 1998, Schedule 1, Part II, para. 10.
7   *Employment Code*, 'Record Management – High Level Management', benchmark 5.

Second, the *Employment Code* also says:[8]

> *Take steps to ensure the reliability of staff that have access to workers'
> records. Remember this is not just a matter of carrying out backgrounds
> checks. It also involves training and ensuring that workers understand
> their responsibilities for confidential or sensitive information. Place
> confidentiality clauses in their contracts of employment.*

In addition to the key element of training on aspects of data protection law, including
the risk of personal liability and the duty of confidentiality, the *Employment Code*
recommends that serious breaches of data protection rules should be a disciplinary
offence.[9]

The *Employment Code* therefore outlines what steps the Information Commissioner
considers reasonable, namely training, disciplinary measures for transgressors of
company policies, procedures and good working practices in relation to data
protection.

DATA CONTROLLERS AND DATA PROCESSORS

The provisions in Part II of Schedule 1 that apply to the seventh principle also legislate
for the relationship between an organisation and third parties that process personal
data on its behalf. This situation may arise when an organisation outsources a function;
for example, an insurance broker that outsources its customer administration, audit
and monitoring functions. The insurance broker is the data controller because the
personal data is processed in accordance with its instructions. The administrator
is a data processor, carrying out the instructions and processing on behalf of the
broker. Another example would be an insurance company that outsources claims
administration to a third party. The insurance company sets the claims handling
criteria but the day-to-day administration, including processing personal data, is
handled on its behalf, by the third party, which is a data processor.

The data controller/data processor relationship also arises between group
companies. Data protection law does not recognise trading groups of companies; each
corporate entity is viewed as a separate data controller and all other corporate entities
are 'third parties' despite ownership in common or branding issues. As a consequence,
when staff are employed by a service company but they actually carry out functions
on behalf of the trading companies, the service company is a data processor and the
trading companies are data controllers for purposes of the seventh principle.

---

8   *Employment Code*, 'Record Management – Security', benchmark 4.
9   *Employment Code*, 'Record Management – High Level Management', benchmark 5.

When organisations set up separate corporate entities on a functional basis this can create anomalies and paradoxes. It may be reasonable for a large business to set up separate subsidiaries, for example, for human resources or information technology, and delegate authority and responsibility on a group-wide basis to those companies. However, the trading companies remain the data controllers, at least in relation to customers, and therefore are obliged to:

- have written contracts between themselves and the functional subsidiary companies;

- monitor the activity of those companies.

By concentrating technical expertise into these functional subsidiaries (the data processors), the data controllers have rendered themselves effectively incapable of independently monitoring the compliance of the data processors. It is unclear what would be regarded as reasonable in these circumstances, but the Act as it stands poses difficult questions over the relationship of companies within the same group.

WHAT IS A 'DATA CONTROLLER'?

A data controller is the entity (organisation, company, club or individual) that makes decisions about the purposes for which personal data is processed (see also Chapter 3). So, for example, a trading company is a data controller of personal data connected with its business, its customers and suppliers. An employing company is data controller of employee personal data. The trustee of a pension scheme is the data controller of personal data relating to past and present members of a pension scheme and their dependants. A charity is the data controller of membership and subscriber lists. A club is the data controller of personal data of its members and so on.

Two or more organisations may be data controllers in relation to the same personal data. For example, an insurance broker is data controller in relation to personal data relating to its clients. As insurance and investments are set up by the broker for its clients, personal data is passed from the broker to product providers. In most cases, the product provider also processes this personal data in the capacity of data controller, rather than as a data processor on behalf of the broker.

Two or more organisations may be joint data controllers in relation to personal data. For example, a prospect marketing database may be jointly owned by two or more companies in a trading group. Each of the joint data controllers is able to determine its own use of the personal data.

WHAT IS A 'DATA PROCESSOR'?

A data processor is an organisation that processes personal data on behalf of the data controller (see also Chapter 3). It provides a service in which it has no interest except the payment it receives for carrying out the work.

The simplest example of a data processor is an outsource service provider such as a payroll administrator. An employer sends payroll data to the payroll administrator at agreed periods and the payroll administrator generates payslips and makes payments into bank accounts on the due date. The payroll administrator has no interest in the personal data per se; it processes the data purely for the benefit of the data controller in return for remuneration. It acts solely on the instructions of the data controller, it has no discretion to act independently and no interest in doing so.

Another example of a data processor would be a debt recovery agent that recovers money from debtors in return for a fee from the principal. Conversely, an organisation involved in debt factoring probably would not be a data processor if the factoring arrangement was an effective sale of the debt so that the factor then acted on its own behalf when recovering the money outstanding. This raises two points. First, the terms 'principal' and 'agent' may help to identify a data controller to data processor relationship. Second, judging when an organisation is acting as a data processor within the meaning of the Act is not always straightforward. It depends on the circumstances.

Identifying data controller to data processor relationships

It is important that data controllers are able to identify their data processor(s) because of the statutory duty of the data controller to comply with the seventh principle. Compliance involves checking that adequate security measures are in place to safeguard the rights and freedoms of data subjects in relation to their personal data and putting appropriate contract terms in place.

A key point is that a data processor will be independent of the data controller. As noted above, the data processor might be described as the agent of the data controller. A data processor is a third party, although it may be a sister or associated company of the data controller in a group of companies. Deciding whether or not a third party is a data processor is a matter of fact. The answers to the following questions will help a data controller to decide whether or not a party is a data processor.

- *Does one party process on the instructions of the other?*
  The data controller is the decision maker as regards the purposes for which personal data will be processed.

● *Does the party process personal data supplied by or on behalf of the data controller?*
  For example, a company might buy a mailing list from a third party and arrange for the list containing personal data to be supplied direct to its preferred mailing house. Although the personal data is not supplied directly by the data controller, it is supplied on its behalf. This does not affect the underlying relationship between the mailing house and the data controller. The mailing house is a data processor on behalf of the data controller.

● *Is the processing undertaken on behalf of or for the benefit of the data controller?*
  Processing undertaken on behalf of the data controller indicates that the relationship is one of data controller to data processor. Processing undertaken for the benefit of the data controller does not necessarily indicate the same relationship.

● *Does the third party have any interest in the personal data apart from remuneration for the service provided to the data controller?*
  If there is a degree of autonomy in the activities of the third party, it is more likely to be a joint data controller than a data processor.

● *Does the third party take decisions in regard to the personal data it processes?*
  The processor may be a data controller in its own right if it uses the personal data for its own purposes or deals with it in any way that would suggest that it is the data controller.

● *What do the parties intend should happen to the personal data when the relationship between them ends?*
  If the party is a data processor then personal data will either be returned to the data controller or its nominated representative or deleted. The data processor will have no further use for the data.

In some cases a service provider may be both data processor and joint data controller. Again, it will depend on the circumstances; for example, a pension fund administrator administers and manages pension schemes on behalf of pension scheme trustees. The administrator acts on the instructions of the trustees generally but those instructions may be worded very widely so that the pension scheme administrator is making decisions relating to the data on a daily basis. In these circumstances the scheme trustees and the scheme administrator are likely to be joint data controllers and, at the same time, the scheme administrator is a data processor on behalf of the trustees.

THE OBLIGATION TO CHECK COMPLIANCE

To discharge its duty under the seventh principle in relation to data processors, the data controller must check the data processor has security measures in place to protect personal data from unauthorised access, deletion or amendment. The seventh principle refers to 'appropriate' security measures, so there is a degree of risk assessment involved. The data controller should assess the risks inherent in the processing based on the type of personal data to be disclosed to the data processor and the processing activity. Then it should assess whether or not the data processor has taken adequate steps to protect personal data in its possession.

The data controller is aware of the type of personal data to be processed and may question a prospective data processor to determine what risks, if any, are inherent in the proposed processing activity. The kind of checks the Information Commissioner would expect a data controller to carry out include requiring the prospective data processor to provide information about its compliance with current data protection law. It should be asked for such details of its security arrangements as it is able to provide without compromising that security. Information should be requested about staff training on data protection issues, how employees are supervised and the controls within which employees work to ensure that they are reliable. This may be particularly important in respect of new employees and temporary workers.

The requirement to ensure that a data processor offers adequate security for the personal data it processes is a continuing requirement. In practical terms a data controller should review compliance when reviewing the performance of its contractor generally. Whether or not there have been any breaches of security will be a key question, together with information about how the breach was handled and the steps taken to ensure that there is no recurrence of that type of breach. A regulated service provider might also be questioned about recent reports to and from its regulator.

THE CONTRACTUAL REQUIREMENT

Where personal data is processed by a data processor on behalf of a data controller, in addition to the duty to ensure that data processors keep personal data securely, the data controller must take specific contractual steps in order to comply with the seventh principle.

The data controller will not be deemed to be compliant with the seventh principle unless there is a written contract in place between the parties incorporating specific terms. The contractual terms required constitute a restriction on the data processor requiring it to act only on instructions from the data controller when processing personal data on the data controller's behalf. There should also be a condition that it comply with obligations equivalent to those imposed on the data controller by the seventh principle.

The impact of the requirement is that organisations must enter into a written contract with subcontractors and service providers where this is not already the case.

Where a contractual relationship already exists between data controller and data processor, the relevant clauses can usually be incorporated into the agreement by exchange of letters, signed on behalf of the data processor to signify its agreement to the amendment.

In addition to the terms specified in the interpretation of the seventh principle, data controllers may find it useful to include a reference in the contract to their obligation to monitor compliance and to establish its right to question security arrangements and any breaches of confidentiality and to gain access to any document it may decide is relevant in that regard.

GROUPS OF COMPANIES AND THE SEVENTH PRINCIPLE

Data protection law does not recognise trading groups of companies. Each company must notify separately and is deemed to be a third party for the purposes of data protection. Therefore companies in a group must consider their relationship with other companies in the group on an 'arm's length' basis. For example, if one company (usually a service company) is the employing company in the group and effectively supplies staff to other, trading companies in the group then it will be a data processor if those staff process personal data in carrying out their job. Consider that most jobs involve handling personal data to some extent, even where this relates to client and supplier representatives in a business-to-business context.

The requirement for written contracts applies as between group companies. However, the Information Commissioner has suggested that such companies seek legal advice on the possibility of entering into one contract with all group companies as signatories in preference to a number of contracts between the service company and each individual trading company.

DATA PROCESSORS OUTSIDE OF UK JURISDICTION

When selecting a data processor located outside of the EEA the data controller must have regard to the eighth principle, which restricts the transfer of personal data outside the EEA. However, the transfer of personal data to a data processor obviously presents less of a compliance risk than a transfer to a data controller, given the degree of control the UK based data controller is required to exert over its data processor and the inherent restrictions imposed by the contract.[10]

The wording of paragraph 12 of the interpretive provisions set out in Part II of Schedule 1 of the Act is that the contract between data processor and data controller should require compliance with obligations equivalent to those imposed on the data

---

10 The contract terms should restrict the data processor to acting only on instructions.

controller by the seventh principle. Where a data processor is located outside the EEA the seventh principle can only apply to its activities by virtue of its relationship with the data controller located within the EEA. The effect of the word 'equivalent' is to place data processors located outside the EEA under the same restriction as UK-based data processors. A data processor may be outside the jurisdiction of the Act but if the data controller is within that jurisdiction, it must ensure that its data processor adheres to security requirements commensurate with those required by the seventh principle regardless of its geographic location.

This is important where a data controller uses the services of data processors located outside the EEA. This aspect is considered in more detail in the next chapter.

RISK MANAGEMENT STRATEGIES

The impact of the seventh principle is to create a need for assessment of the security risk posed by and to all personal data processing activities. Having identified the risks, appropriate security measures should be put in place based on the degree of risk identified, 'state of the art' technological developments and the cost of implementation.

Organisational security measures will rely in part on documenting policies and procedures with security features such as clean desk policies, use of confidential shredding facilities, and so on. Staff training and communication of policies and procedures is a necessary corollary once procedures are established. The Information Commissioner would expect data controllers to carry out regular audits to ensure that policies and procedures are adequate and practical and that they are being followed in practice.

To meet the specific requirements in relation to outsourced functions, data controllers should identify their existing data processors and those circumstances where a data controller to data processor relationship is likely to arise. In the latter cases and when existing contracts are put out to tender, the selection process should include careful vetting of prospective data processors to check that system and organisational security measures are adequate. There is a significant overlap with business requirements in this respect; organisations will require a degree of security and confidentiality from outsource service providers regardless of the requirements of the Act. The key to compliance is, as ever, to document the checks carried out.

Written contracts are required with all data processors. The terms of the contract must include a requirement that the data processor act only on the instructions of the data controller in relation to processing personal data and that it adhere to the seventh data protection principle. The Legal Department should be briefed to double check each draft contract for whether the relationship is one to which the seventh principle applies.

On a continuing basis the data controller should monitor the data processor's performance in relation to security.

CONCLUSION

There are three key elements to the seventh principle. First, the requirement for appropriate security measures for personal data processed by the organisation. Second, ensuring the reliability of staff whose job brings them into contact with personal data. Third, identifying and monitoring the compliance of data processors with the obligations relating to security imposed by the principle.

Maintaining appropriate levels of organisational security depends heavily on policies and procedures and good working practices. However, these are only effective if they are practical and realistic, communicated properly to all staff, and policed. In particular, for the data controller to be able to demonstrate that policies and procedures are being followed, audit is an important tool. Audit will also reveal which procedures are impractical or inappropriate.

The importance of training for staff whose role brings them into contact with personal data is stressed in the *Employment Code*. Training is essential for staff required to follow policies and procedures when handling personal data. Understanding the principles of data protection and the reasons why policies and procedures exist will, in turn, help staff to remember relevant procedures and apply them.

Identifying and monitoring data processors is a continuing requirement. An audit may help to identify data processors at a given point in time but staff need training to help them to recognise when the obligations under the seventh principle are likely to be relevant with outsourcing, appointment of agents and using service providers.

CHAPTER 10

The Eighth Principle

Personal data shall not be transferred to a country or territory outside the European Economic Area unless that country or territory ensures an adequate level of protection for the rights and freedoms of data subjects in relation to the processing of personal data.

The eighth principle gives effect to Article 25 of the Data Protection Directive.[1] The directive provides that EU member states should legislate for a restriction on the transfer of personal data to third countries so that such transfers might take place only if the third country ensures an adequate level of protection for the rights and freedoms of data subjects in relation to personal data processing. The Data Protection Directive defines third countries as non-EU member states, although this is extended in the UK version of the eighth principle to countries in the EEA.

WHAT IS A 'TRANSFER'?

The accepted view is that a transfer is not the same as transit.[2] Data in transit through one country en route to a different destination country is not deemed to be 'transferred' to the intermediate country.

The view of the Information Commissioner in the 2000 guidance is that the publication of personal data on a website will almost certainly involve transfer to countries outside the UK,[3] although there is a problem in that the transfer does not take place until the web pages are accessed from a transferee country. However, since the European Court of Justice (ECJ) decision in the Lindqvist[4] case it is arguable whether or not the publication of personal data on a website constitutes a transfer. Mrs Lindqvist was an active church parishioner in Sweden. To disseminate information of interest to other parishioners, Mrs Lindqvist set up an Internet website. Included on the website were personal details relating to fellow parishioners and Mrs Lindqvist was found to be processing personal data in breach of Swedish data protection law. One of the points in issue was whether or not the publication of personal data on the website

1   EC Directive 95/46/EC.
2   Information Commissioner (2000) *International Transfers of Personal Data*, para. 4.1 and Information Commissioner (1999) *The Eighth Data Protection Principle and Transborder Dataflows*. London: Data Protection Registrar, para. 4.1.
3   *International Transfers of Personal Data*, para. 4.3.
4   *Bodil Lindqvist* v. *Kammeraklagareu* [2003] C101/01 ECJ6/11/2003.

amounted to a worldwide transfer. The ECJ held that publishing personal data on the website did not amount to a worldwide transfer; it would be a transfer only if the information was sent to Internet users who did not intentionally seek access to the website pages. Most authorities think this decision is wrong and it should be treated as an aberration.

A PROHIBITION ON TRANSFERS OUTSIDE THE EEA

Countries within the EEA are deemed to have an adequate level of protection for personal data. The Directive on Data Protection[5] set the basic requirements for processing personal data so that it is transferable throughout the EU. In addition, the three countries in the EEA but not in the EU, Norway, Liechtenstein and Iceland, are also deemed to offer adequate protection for personal data.

The Directive on Data Protection provides for third countries (that is countries outside the EEA) to be designated by the EC as providing an adequate level of protection for the rights and freedoms of data subjects in relation to their personal data. To date, Argentina, Canada, Guernsey, Hungary,[6] Isle of Man and Switzerland have been designated as providing adequate data protection. Transfers of personal data to these countries may be effected without further checks as to adequacy or exemptions.

The USA does not have a data protection regime that would qualify for such wholesale approval, but Safe Harbor, a voluntary data protection code for individual organisations to embrace, has been approved by the EC as providing an adequate level of protection, so any organisation that subscribes to Safe Harbor is deemed to provide adequate data protection.

The EC is under a duty to police its decisions of adequacy and its recent review of Safe Harbor arrangements in the USA has revealed some problems.[7] The prime requirement for US organisations signing up to Safe Harbor is a public statement that they adhere to a set of data protection 'principles'. The public statement triggers the Federal Trade Commission's (FTC) authority to enforce the principles and, without it, the FTC does not have authority to regulate compliance with the Safe Harbor provisions. The report found that many organisations were not making the required public statement. The report also noted disappointingly low take-up of the Safe Harbor protocol among companies in the USA; around 400 have signed up to date.

---

5   EC Directive 95/46/EC.
6   As it has now joined the EC, Hungary qualifies for authorised personal data transfers as a member state.
7   Report by Article 29 working party. Available at
    www.europa.eu.int/comm/justice_home/fsj/privacy/workinggroup/index_en.htm.

COUNTRIES WITHIN THE EEA

The following are countries currently within the EEA.

Austria	Hungary	Netherlands
Belgium	Iceland	Norway
Cyprus	Ireland	Poland
Czech Republic	Italy	Portugal
Denmark	Latvia	Slovakia
Estonia	Liechtenstein	Slovenia
Finland	Lithuania	Spain
France	Luxembourg	Sweden
Germany	Malta	UK
Greece		

The Channel Islands and the Isle of Man are not part of the EEA.

EXCEPTIONS TO THE PROHIBITION

In practice, there are exceptions that might take personal data outside of the prohibition. These exceptions cover specific circumstances set out in Schedule 4 to the Data Protection Act 1998 (the Act). Where an exemption applies the prohibition on the transfer of personal data outside the EEA is lifted. The more commonly applicable conditions are considered below.

CONSENT

A data subject may consent to the transfer of personal data relating to themselves notwithstanding that the transfer takes the personal data outside of the EEA. Consent must be an informed, freely given, indication of agreement. The fact of the transfer and that protection for the rights of the data subject may not meet standards within the EEA must be communicated.

Guidance from the Information Commissioner indicates that consent should be the last resort; data controllers should always consider other conditions as authority to process personal data before relying on consent.[8]

---

8   *Legal Guidance*, para. 3.1.5.

For consent to be informed, specific and unambiguous, the details of the transfer must be ascertained, that is, it must be clear and communicable exactly which third countries are involved, that a data transfer will take place and the type of data to be transferred. Consent may also operate to make the authority effectively time restricted. A general consent to the global transfer of data will not be effective, as it will not be specific. However, the advantage offered by consent as authority for a transfer outside of the EEA is that it applies in most circumstances. The remaining derogations apply in limited circumstances.

The circumstances in which consent may not operate effectively is as between employee and employer. It is now doubtful that proper consent can be given by the employee to the processing of personal data relating to them by the employer. The view has been expressed that in the relationship between employer and employee, the employee is at such a disadvantage in terms of bargaining power, that they cannot ever give consent freely and without undue influence from the employer, simply by virtue of the fact that this is the employer. The Information Commissioner has indicated agreement with this view.

WHERE THE DATA SUBJECT IS PARTY TO A CONTRACT

A key exception to the general prohibition on the transfer of personal data outside the EEA is where the transfer is necessary for the performance of a contract between the data subject and the data controller. The exception also applies where steps are taken at the request of the data subject with a view to their entering into a contract with the data controller.

Generally this condition will apply to any transfers required pursuant to a contract of employment, for example. If a transfer of employee personal data is necessary for the administration of employee benefits and the transferee is located in a territory outside the EEA, the transfer may be made despite the eighth principle. However, the transfer must be truly necessary. If an organisation chooses to base its administrative functions outside the EEA, it will not be able to argue necessity for the transfer to it of employee personal data, the location of the administration function in these circumstances being a matter of choice rather than necessity. This is an issue that has been highlighted by the recent trend towards locating administrative functions in third countries where labour costs are cheaper than in the UK; for example, outsourcing call centres or document archive and management facilities to India.

This restricted interpretation[9] of what is necessary has other implications. Applying the same logic, arguably if the objectives of a contract could be achieved without transferring personal data outside the EEA, then the transfer is unnecessary and

---

9   *International Transfers of Personal Data*, para. 8.3.

fails to meet the criteria of necessity and therefore the Schedule 4 condition. An illustration in the insurance context is helpful. If a broker seeks terms for insurance for a client, should it be restricted to underwriters located in the EEA and prevented from approaching non-EEA underwriters? If terms can be put forward by an EEA underwriter, then how may the broker justify approaching underwriters outside the EEA if that approach involves the disclosure of personal data? It appears that it may not be possible for the contract condition to be relied upon in these circumstances.

Other cases where the contractual authorisation for a transfer of personal data outside the EEA is likely to be ineffective are those where the transferor is not the data controller, for example where an intermediary is involved. In such cases it will be a matter of fact as to whether the intermediary is a joint controller or simply the agent of the controller when making the transfer. As an agent, the intermediary is covered by the authority of its principal, the controller. As a joint controller, the intermediary will probably not be a party to the eventual contract with the data subject and so cannot take advantage of the contract with the data subject as authority for the transfer.

APPROVED CONTRACT TERMS

Another key condition for authorising transfers of personal data to countries located outside the EEA is where the transfer is made on approved contract terms. The EC has to have approved the terms and the first set of terms were approved and published in 2001.[10] Practitioners and corporates alike have reported problems with the terms being too prescriptive and inflexible. Early in 2005 new standard contractual clauses were approved and published specifically to regulate transfers of personal data to data controllers located in third countries. In January 2005, the EC also announced that it was working on new standard contractual clauses so that personal data can be transferred from a data controller established in any of the EU member states to a data processor established in a country not ensuring an adequate level of data protection.

BINDING CORPORATE RULES

One of the ways in which organisations seeking to transfer personal data from within the EU to a country located outside the EEA (a 'third country') might legitimise the transfer is to seek approval of contract terms from its national data protection authority pursuant to Article 26(2) of the EU Data Protection Directive.

In a working document adopted on 3 June 2003,[11] the Article 29 Working Party set out guidance on 'binding corporate rules'. Entitled 'Binding Corporate Rules for International Data Transfers', the working document gives guidance on how national authorities might consider approving a self-regulatory approach for multinational

---

10 See www.europa.eu.int/comm/justice_home/fsj/privacy/index_en.htm.
11 See www.europa.eu.int/comm/justice_home/fsj/privacy/index_en.htm.

companies. It also starts to lay the foundations for cooperation between national data protection authorities when considering data protection compliance of an organisation with operations in more than one EU member state.

Key elements identified by the Article 29 Working Party were that an intra-group code of conduct should be binding or legally enforceable and that it should comprise rules that apply to multinational organisations and that facilitate international data transfers.

In April 2005, the Article 29 Working Party adopted a 'Working Document Establishing a Model Checklist Application for Approval of Binding Corporate Rules'. The checklist sets out the required information to be submitted to a national data protection authority for consideration under Article 26(2) and explains why each piece of information is required. be adopted by the organisation. As well as a general statement of principle, the data protection authorities need to see how personal data is actually handled within the group.

LEGAL CLAIMS

Transfers of personal data to parties located outside the EEA may be made where the transfer is necessary in connection with any legal proceedings. This exception includes prospective legal proceedings, obtaining legal advice or establishing, exercising or defending legal rights.

There is no requirement that the data subject be a party to the legal proceedings or prospective legal proceedings. However, there is still the proviso that the transfer must be 'necessary' for the purposes; so, for example it would be permissible to take a written report to the USA to use as part of a witness statement in a US Court when required by law to do so but it would not be permissible to take written reports to the USA to consult with US lawyers if legal advice could be obtained in the UK.

ASSESSING ADEQUACY

If none of the conditions in Schedule 4 to the Act applies and the country of the intended transfer of the personal data has not been presumed adequate by the EC, the data controller must make its own assessment of adequacy. The adequacy of protection for data subjects' rights and freedoms in relation to data protection must be made both in respect of the territory where the transferee is located and as offered by the transferee organisation.

Certain circumstances may help to establish adequacy; for example, if the transfer is one between a data controller and its data processor and an appropriate contract is in place to meet the requirements of the seventh principle. If the transfer is being made within an industry sector where professional rules or a code of conduct apply, this may also be factored into the assessment of adequacy. The Information Commissioner pointed out that these circumstances in themselves could not be relied on completely to establish adequacy but that they would count in favour of (or against) a final assessment of adequacy.[12]

THE ADEQUACY TEST

The factors relevant to a decision about adequacy are set out in Part II of Schedule 1 to the Act, the interpretive provisions relating to the data protection principles, which state:

> *An adequate level of protection is one which is adequate in all the circumstances of the case, having regard in particular to –*
>
> *a)   the nature of the personal data,*
>
> *b)   the country or territory of origin of the information contained in the data,*
>
> *c)   the country or territory of final destination of that information,*
>
> *d)   the purposes for which and period during which the data are intended to be processed,*
>
> *e)   the law in force in the country or territory in question,*
>
> *f)   the international obligations of that country or territory,*
>
> *g)   any relevant codes of conduct or other rules which are enforceable in that country or territory (whether generally or by arrangement in particular cases), and*
>
> *h)   any security measures taken in respect of the data in that country or territory.*[13]

The Information Commissioner has issued guidance setting out a recommended procedure to assess adequacy.[14] The test is to be applied if a proposed transfer does not fall within one of the exceptions in Schedule 4 to the Act and the transfer is to an organisation located in a territory which has not been approved by the EC. In these circumstances, the following measures are considered the 'good practice' approach:

● Consider the type of transfer involved and whether this assists in determining adequacy: for example, if the transfer is within an industry sector where professional rules or standards apply (underwriters for example) or is a transfer within an international group of companies. Although this will not establish adequacy prima facie, it may go some way

---

12 *Transborder Dataflows*, para. 11.5.
13 The Data Protection Act 1998, Schedule 1, Part II, para. 13.
14 *Transborder Dataflows*.

towards it because the data controller has a level of knowledge about the security and procedures within the transferee company and may have an ongoing relationship that both parties wish to protect.

● Consider:

  – the nature of the personal data (consider sensitive personal data in, particular);

  – the country or territory of origin of the personal data;

  – the purposes for which and period during which the data are intended to be processed;

  – the harm that might result from improper processing;

  – the law in force in the country or territory in question;

  – the international obligations of that country or territory;

  – any relevant codes of conduct or other rules that are enforceable in the country or territory;

  – any security measures taken in respect of the data in that country or territory;

  – the extent to which data protection standards have been adopted;

  – whether there is a means of ensuring the standards are achieved in practice; and

  – whether there is an effective mechanism for individuals to enforce their rights or obtain redress if things go wrong.

● Think whether there are any circumstances in your knowledge or that of others involved in the proposed transfer, which put you on notice that it is not appropriate to make the data transfer; for example, if the organisation is aware of breaches of confidentiality at the transferee company or other data security problems.

As a matter of principle there are two major issues with this adequacy test. First, the prospective transferor takes full responsibility when deciding whether or not the third country and the organisation receiving the transfer offer an adequate level of protection for data transferred. The final decision will be subjective and there is every possibility that it will be made by a designated individual, putting significant pressure onto that individual. Second, it is a critical decision and, if undertaken properly, will utilise key resources in assessing the circumstances of the proposed transfer equating to time and money.

There are other practical problems with making an assessment of adequacy. The adequacy test is couched in terms of prospective transferors establishing the adequacy of data protection at national level in the third country (like Article 25(2) of the EC Directive on which it is based).[15] Most organisations have links with other organisations rather than with national governments and their assessment of the legal structure will rely heavily on information provided by the prospective transferee. Prospective transferees in third countries whose data protection laws set a much lower standard (or none at all) than those in the EU will not understand the need to establish their data protection credentials simply because they will not understand the issues, having no similar laws for comparison. Therefore prospective transferors to third countries with a lower standard of data protection will have the hardest time gathering information to carry out the adequacy test.

The adequacy test is an inappropriate route for organisations wishing either to transfer personal data to a large number of organisations located in third countries or to make regular transfers of personal data to organisations located in third countries. It is basically a method of authorising one-off transfers of data.

USE OF CONTRACTS

In addition, contractual terms may be used to supplement the security of personal data transfers. The Directive specifically provides for contract terms to be used in this way; however, the usefulness of this provision is significantly restricted by the fact that the contract terms must be in a form approved by the EC, as noted above.

Unless an organisation is able to use the model terms approved by the EC, it is unlikely that a non-standard contract (that is, one not approved in full by the EC or the Information Commissioner) would legitimise a transfer of personal data outside the EEA without the adequacy test risk assessment yielding a positive result in addition.

The issues you should seek to cover in a non-standard contract are:

- purpose limitation – restricting the purpose(s) for which the personal data supplied can be processed;

- security – requiring appropriate technical and organisational security measures be taken by the disclosee;

- restrictions on onward transfers;

- additional safeguards for sensitive personal data.

---

15 EC Directive 95/46/EC.

BECOMING AWARE OF INADEQUATE PROTECTION

Even if the transfer has been justified by one of the conditions of Schedule 4 to the Act, is being made to an approved territory or is being made following a positive adequacy finding, consider whether there are any circumstances in your knowledge or that of others involved in the proposed transfer, which put you on notice that it is not appropriate to make the data transfer. For example, if you are aware of breaches of confidentiality at the transferee company or other data security problems, any transfer of personal data may be in breach of the eighth principle.

SUMMARY

- Transfers within the EEA are authorised.

- Transfers to countries that have been approved by the EC are likewise authorised, currently Argentina, Canada, Guernsey and Switzerland.

- Transfers to the USA to companies that subscribe to Safe Harbor are approved.

- Other transfers must be authorised by the adequacy test unless one of the conditions in Schedule 4 to the Act is met.

The key problems when undertaking personal data transfers outside of the EEA are that the derogations are either limited in application with many prospective transferors unable to take advantage of them, or the terms of the derogation are difficult to comply with. The potentially most generally applicable derogation, transfers undertaken on contractual terms, has had its value eroded by the specific requirement for such terms to be approved by the EC together with the prescriptive nature of the terms so approved for global data transfers.

The adequacy test is the only option for many prospective transferors, but this involves the allocation of resources to check all the relevant circumstances described and applies on an individual transfer basis rather than accommodating mass transfers.

PART II

Key Implications Relating to the Stages of the Financial Services' Customer Life Cycle

The following chapters take their structure from an average customer life cycle. We start with advertising messages in Chapter 12 and marketing and privacy issues are considered in Chapter 13. Chapter 14 looks at the third principle in the context of the sale process, that is the requirement for personal data to be adequate, relevant and not excessive. Chapter 15 looks at the implications of handling sensitive categories of data, Chapter 16 focuses on the implications of creating customer records and Chapter 17 on the security requirements for those records. Chapter 18 considers how an organisation might respond to the exercise of subject rights under the Data Protection Act 1998 during the currency of a relationship with a customer. Finally, Chapter 19 looks at the topical issues surrounding outsourcing administration work to India.

CHAPTER 11

What Is Personal Data?

In 2004 the Information Commissioner commissioned research into the question 'What is personal data?'. The report[1] considered several aspects of the question. First, the sociological issues were identified as our fears arising from modernity, bureaucracy and the use of information by organisations and the state. Our fears also relate to social control and surveillance, the identification and accountability of individuals and how these might be used to serve the interests of the powerful.

The second aspect is the psychological one. A person's need for privacy is a key factor in the relationship between the individual and the environment. Privacy is seen as helping to establish an identity of place and a sense of belonging.

The third aspect is the legal one. It was noted that although data protection regulation throughout the European Union (EU) is based on the EC Directive on Data Protection[2] there are significant differences in the way it has been implemented. The legal definition of personal data in the Directive[3] refers to 'information relating to an identified or identifiable natural person' where an identifiable person is one 'who can be identified, directly or indirectly, in particular by reference to an identification number or to one or more factors specific to his physical, physiological, mental, economic, cultural or social identity'. One issue arising is whether or not a 'natural person' includes a deceased person; for example, in the UK it does not, but in Portugal it does.

A key divergence in the implementation of the Directive is the interpretation of what is 'identifiable' with an individual. One premise is that it is any information that allows an individual to be identified; this is a narrow definition and overlooks the inclusion of 'indirect' information which is specified in the definition in the Directive. Another premise is that the information concerns an individual or their interests. This is a very wide definition and includes potentially almost all data. In particular it would not be possible to anonymise personal data following this second interpretation. The conclusion of the report was that there was no consistency in the classification of types of data into personal and non-personal data across jurisdictions within and outside

---

1 University of Sheffield (2004) *What are 'Personal Data'?* A study conducted for the UK Information Commissioner, University of Sheffield, 2004. Available from www.informationcommissioner.gov.uk.
2 Directive 95/46/EC.
3 Article 2.

of the EU. Three main groupings were made of how different jurisdictions defined 'personal data', that is, those that implemented data protection law on the premise that:

- information can only be personal data if it can identify an individual;

- personal data must relate to an identifiable individual but does not necessarily identify the individual, it may simply relate to them;

- personal data is information that both clearly identifies and clearly affects the individual's privacy.

The UK's position based on the Data Protection Act 1998, as interpreted by the Information Commissioner (through all three holders of the position and all of its different names), was closest to the widest definition, that is information that relates to an identifiable individual but which does not necessarily identify them. However, there was a Court of Appeal decision in a recent, landmark case,[4] which made significant changes to the way data protection law is applied in the UK. It narrowed the definition of 'personal data' so that we now apply a definition similar to the third premise, that is, information that both clearly identifies and clearly affects the individual's privacy.

Even taking into account this narrower interpretation of what constitutes personal data, it is clear that much of the information required by financial services organisations in relation to individual clients and customers falls within the definition.

In conclusion, personal data is information relating to people. It is information that is biographical and which features them as the subject matter of the file, document or report. Most financial services operations handle personal data relating to consumers, with the exception of corporate and institutional investments and reinsurance contracts. Even corporate bankers and institutional investment houses use personal data to contact colleagues and representatives at other organisations and for employee administration purposes. So all organisations in the financial services sector are affected by data protection law. The impact of that law on the activities of financial services operations is considered in the chapters that follow.

---

4   *Durant* v. *Financial Services Authority* [2003] EWCA Civ 1746.

CHAPTER 12

Advertising and the Impact of the First and Second Principles

This chapter considers the data protection issues that arise when non-targeted promotions are undertaken. 'Non-targeted' in this context, is taken to mean a promotion that does not involve the use of personal information. Nevertheless, any promotion offers an opportunity to start to communicate the organisation's policy on data protection. Initially the appropriate message may simply be an indication that the organisation takes seriously issues of confidentiality and security. In addition, data protection statements can include important information required by data protection law, such as the name of the party that controls the use of personal data. In most cases this will be the advertiser, but not necessarily. The status of the organisation can affect whether or not it is the 'controller' of personal information. Three roles have been identified as relevant: product provider, intermediary and affinity advertiser. The data protection implications for each when inviting prospective customers to contact them for further product information are considered below.

NON-TARGETED PROMOTIONS

'Non-targeted promotions' are advertising that does not involve the use of personal data; for example, posters, radio and television advertisements, leaflets available to be picked up from branch offices, newspaper and magazine advertisements and websites. All these media provide an opportunity for the organisation to communicate with as yet unidentified, prospective enquirers and existing customers. The key message usually relates to a product or service or focus on raising brand awareness, but non-targeted promotions also communicate messages about the organisation and its values. The tone of the advertisement conveys, for example, whether the organisation and/or its products and services are 'cheap and cheerful' or 'exclusive' and 'expensive'.

Any form of communication with prospects and customers presents an opportunity to inform about data protection policies. For many organisations, particularly in the financial services sector, processing personal information is a key element of the service provided; for example, pension administrators process personal information relating to pension scheme members, pensioners and beneficiaries. Independent financial advisers 'fact-find' personal information in order to be able to advise clients on appropriate financial products. In the financial services sector, an organisation's privacy or data protection policy should be seen as a key selling point, an issue on which to reassure prospects and existing customers alike.

There is also a good legal reason for using non-targeted advertisements to provide information about data protection policies. The first principle includes the requirement to provide information about the organisation and the purposes for which personal information will be processed. The timing of providing this information is critical. Where personal information is obtained direct from the individual, for example, a response to a website enquiry form or an off-the-page coupon, advertisers must provide the required information before any personal information is obtained. The need to provide subject information is one of the reasons for the recent proliferation of privacy policies on corporate websites. Advertisers are seeking to put their data protection message across to browsers and meet subject information requirements in a friendly and accessible way.

Not all advertisements are appropriate vehicles for data protection statements of policy. Advertisers should consider whether the medium to be used for the advertisement lends itself to a data protection statement. Radio advertisements and posters probably do not. Spoken compliance messages sound clumsy and use of creative space is an issue when considering whether to include lengthy wording on posters. Nonetheless, depending on the sensitivity of the product or service advertised, simple words like 'confidentiality' or 'privacy' can be reassuring and a key part of the advertising message. At the same time, such words start to convey the organisation's attitude to data protection and will be binding on the organisation. So, if your organisation promises absolute confidentiality, it had better make sure that its procedures and staff training are adequate to deliver it.

For those advertisements where space is not an issue, an appropriate privacy policy adds value to the messages conveyed. With increasing consumer awareness of privacy issues and given the nature of financial services generally, communications about privacy, security and fair processing are appropriate messages.

In some circumstances it is essential to provide subject information, as no further opportunity will be afforded the advertiser before prospects submit their personal information. If an off-the-page coupon is part of the advertisement or online applications are accepted, the advertisement must feature the information required.

SUBJECT INFORMATION – WHAT IS REQUIRED?

Subject information required by data protection law comprises:

- the name of the organisation collecting the personal data;

- the purposes for which that data will be processed;

- any other information relevant in the circumstances.

As noted in Chapter 4 on the first data protection principle, information relevant in the circumstances will almost certainly be impacted by the status of the organisation; for example, an intermediary will pass on information collected to a product provider and that onward disclosure is relevant in the circumstances of the customer's enquiry.

It will include any prospective disclosures of the information and any consequences of supplying, or even not supplying, the information requested. In particular, it should include any unusual circumstances that might affect an individual's decision to provide personal information as requested. Obviously this will depend on the circumstances; for example, material non-disclosure of relevant information in an insurance proposal can invalidate the eventual policy and is a key fact that should be made known to the proposer when they are providing personal information in the proposal form.

The information required is probably already included in most advertisements. An advertisement usually gives the name of the advertiser, even if this is represented in the form of a logo. If an organisation conveys its identity through its logo, it can be useful to register any words that form part of the logo as a trading style on the Data Protection Register to assist enquirers to locate the relevant register entry. The purposes for which personal information is intended to be processed at the enquiry stage are also fairly self-evident and usually stated in the advertisement – 'contact us for further information' on a coupon is a clear indication that name and address details will be used to provide the further information sought. The danger is that any other, non-obvious purposes for which personal information might be processed, such as further marketing activity or screening for suitability for the advertised product, will not be covered by such a statement.

Marketing activities are subject to more rigorous requirements than other personal data processing activities. In the UK it is accepted practice to offer prospective marketing targets an opt-out, the chance to decline to receive further targeted marketing material from the advertiser. Opt-out clauses are frequently positioned with or near subject information. Successive data protection regulators have indicated their support for the standard set out in the British Codes of Advertising and Sales

Promotion[1] which require that individuals be given the opportunity to object to the use of their personal data for marketing purposes (the marketing opt-out rather than the higher standard of opt-in). The marketing opt-out is the standard in the *DM Code of Practice*. In the UK this is accepted as a requirement to make processing of personal data for marketing purposes fair.

If the advertiser is one of a group of companies, it may be standard practice to share personal data with other companies in the group. This is information that must be included in subject information. The usual reason for sharing data within a group of companies is for marketing purposes, so that other products and services available from the group can be promoted to the individual.

ISSUES FOR PRODUCT PROVIDERS, INTERMEDIARIES AND AFFINITY MARKETERS

Regardless of the role of the advertiser, the data protection issues are the same. There is a requirement to meet subject information provisions where personal data is sought on a coupon or website enquiry form. The advertiser may choose to include subject information on other advertisements if space and the medium of the advertisement permit. However, the status and role of the advertiser will impact on issues around ownership of the customer and this, in turn, has data protection implications.

Assuming that an advertiser decides to include subject information in its non-targeted advertisement, one of the data-flows it must consider is the disclosure of personal data to third parties. This is information that should be included in subject information. The role of the advertiser will impact on the likely disclosures; for example, an intermediary will disclose personal data to the product provider, and an affinity marketer may disclose personal data to a product provider, or an intermediary, or both. Appropriate wording should indicate that personal data will be disclosed to product providers and their agents.

Where a product provider elects to outsource some of its functions there is not necessarily a disclosure of personal data. It will depend on the circumstances, but in general outsourcing is treated differently in data protection law to a disclosure to another party acting as principal. Provided that it is functionality that is being outsourced rather than decision making and the outsource service provider is acting at all times on the instructions of the principal and on contract terms that meet data protection requirements,[2] there is no disclosure of personal data. The outsource service provider is not acting as a principal and this is key in data protection terms. This

---

1   Advertising Standards Authority (2003) *British Code of Advertising, Sales Promotion and Direct Marketing* (11th edition). London: ASA.
2   See Chapter 10 on the seventh principle.

is also the case where a regulated broker firm outsources its administration and audit functions to a service provider. The processing of data by the service provider does not constitute a disclosure for data protection purposes because it is not acting as the principal when processing the personal data. Note, however, that there are significant data protection requirements to regulate that particular outsourcing arrangement, including appropriate contract terms in writing.

Marketing in an environment where intermediaries, product providers and outsource service providers all operate raises issues around ownership of the customer. Intermediaries are generally accepted as 'owning' their clients and customers. They provide advice on appropriate products and shop around to find the best terms for the best price. Each year, the intermediary expects to re-market the risk and may advise their client to change product providers where this is appropriate, for example with insurance, loan or mortgage.

Where the product provider has direct access to the customer, either through direct marketing or in the administration process for an intermediary sale, it may include in subject information its right to market to the individual. The only way for the intermediary to prevent this is to prohibit the product provider from approaching customers in the terms of business between the parties. Given that the intermediary is likely to be a smaller organisation than the product provider for reasons outlined above, inequality of bargaining positions will affect whether or not it is possible for the intermediary to restrict the marketing activities of the product provider in relation to its referrals.

Employee 'save as you earn' share schemes provide a good example of outsourcing and the changing roles of parties involved. The share options are granted by the employer or another company in the employer's group of companies. The terms of the offer require individuals to open a building society account with a chosen building society and save a regular amount for a period of years. The employer is not authorised to accept deposits and must arrange this functionality via a bank or building society. Assuming that the names of new employees eligible to participate in the scheme are passed to the building society for them to arrange the invitation and application pack, the disclosure of those names is an outsourcing function. There is no intention that the building society obtain the right to market to those individuals who decline to participate in the scheme or who simply do not reply to the invitation. Provided the appropriate contract terms are in place, the building society acts at all times on the instructions of the employer. It is important from the employer's viewpoint that appropriate contract terms are in place, otherwise it will have made an unlawful disclosure of employee personal data.[3]

---

3   See Chapter 10 on the seventh principle.

Continuing this example, the invitation and application pack for participation in an employee share scheme will include an application form to open an account with the building society. It will be a standard form with subject information including the marketing opt-out. Once the prospective participant completes the form, they become the building society's customer and the building society has the right to promote its other services or not, depending on the opt-out clause.

EXAMPLES OF SUBJECT INFORMATION

The simplest use of personal data is where a non-targeted promotion has attracted the interest of a prospect who then follows up the advertisement by making contact with the advertiser. At that point, the prospect is asked for name and contact details so that an application pack can be sent to them. Name and contact details constitute personal information, so a short subject information statement explaining the use of personal details for communication purposes is all that is required.

A subject information statement should identify the organisation that intends to create a record of the personal information and should explain why the information is required and how it will be used and disclosed. Many sale processes involve more than one stage, so there will be subsequent opportunities to provide more detailed subject information describing administrative processes. Here we focus on promotional activity, so we assume that we are creating leads, inviting prospects to contact the organisation for further information about the product or service advertised, for example, when liaising direct with consumers:

> *The information we, [name of business or company], require will be used for the purposes of providing a personalised illustration of the chosen product. Your details will be kept confidential.*

As the individual has specifically requested the product information, there is no need for a marketing opt-out clause unless it is intended to use the name and contact details again in relation to another marketing initiative. In the case where further marketing activity is intended, the following clause would be appropriate:

> *The information we, [name of business or company], require will be used for the purposes of providing a personalised illustration of the chosen product. We would like to keep you advised of our other products and services. If you do not wish to receive such information please tick this box. Your personal details will be kept confidential.*

Or if the marketer is likely to be a third party:

> *The information we, [name of business or company], require will be used for the purposes of providing a personalised illustration of the chosen*

product. We will share your information with [name] our sister company for marketing purposes. If you do not wish to receive details of our products and services please tick this box. If you do not wish to receive details of products and services provided by our sister company please tick this box. Your personal details will be kept confidential.

WHY SUBJECT INFORMATION IS CRITICAL

The first data protection principle states that personal data will be processed fairly and lawfully and, in particular, that fairness involves providing specified information to individuals before their personal data is processed.

If processing is judged to be unfair and therefore in breach of the first principle, there are ramifications, not just in terms of data protection enforcement activity.[4] The organisation loses its authority to process the personal information and it must be deleted or the consent of the individuals to whom it relates must be sought in order to regain the authority to process.

The second implication of statements of subject information is that they are binding on the organisation in terms of its future processing activity. Subject information specifies the purposes for which the organisation intends to process personal data and its authority to process is then restricted to the purposes so described. This is derived from the second principle, which states that personal data will be obtained only for specified purposes and shall not be processed in any manner incompatible with those purposes.[5]

To illustrate the point, the example involving the use of the electoral roll is useful. The electoral roll is maintained by local registrars and is recognised as comprising information in the public domain, accessible to all. From time to time, marketers have used the electoral roll as a marketing database. The Information Commissioner considered this use of the electoral roll and decided that it was not compatible with the purposes for which it had been established, namely to record voters in each ward. The use of personal information on the electoral roll for marketing was judged to be unfair; however, registrars are still required to make the electoral roll available on request. It is now supplied subject to restrictions on its use for marketing purposes. If information on the electoral roll were to be used for marketing, then a marketing opt-out clause would be required. Consequently, the electoral roll is now maintained with additional fields to show who has and who has not opted out of marketing activity.

---

4   See Chapter 4 on the first principle.
5   See Chapter 5 on the second principle.

SPECIAL RULES FOR WEBSITES

The same requirement to provide subject information applies to websites where visitors are invited to submit any personal information. Simply using the 'contact us' facility often generates a return email address regardless of the further content of the email. In guidance,[6] the Information Commissioner has said that a privacy statement will not always suffice for these purposes if it is in the form of 'click here to view our privacy statement'. Instead, the key subject information should be provided at any point where personal information is collected online.

The DMA advises its members that a privacy policy should be accessible in one click of a mouse via a prominently flagged link. It should not be one link among many nor should it be a referral to general terms and conditions. The link should be easy to locate and on the top part of the page visible on screen, preferably not in a list of links at the side, or visible only when the user has scrolled to the bottom of the page.[7]

Websites are also subject to the Electronic Commerce (EC Directive) Regulations 2002[8] (based on the E-Commerce Directive[9]), which came into effect in October 2003. The regulations apply to any organisation (or person) that advertises goods or services online or sells goods or services to businesses or consumers online.

The main requirements relate to information that must be provided on a website. A website should include:

- clear contact details for the website owner, including a geographical address;

- an explanation of any cookies used on or by the website, their function and purpose;

- a facility for individuals to opt out of the use of cookies;

- clear price indications for products available to purchase over the Internet;

- the advertiser's VAT number where products are available to purchase over the Internet;

- details of how contracts will be made online;

- details of any relevant trade organisations to which the advertiser belongs or any authority to conduct business.

---

6 Compliance advice, Website Frequently Asked Questions, 26 June 2001. Available from www.informationcommissioner.gov.uk.

7 Direct Marketing Association (2004) *Email Marketing Council, Best Practice Guidelines.* Available from www.dma.org.uk/DocFrame/DocView.asp?id=230.

8 EC Directive SI 2002 No. 2013.

9 EC Directive 2000/31/EC.

Failure to comply with the Electronic Commerce Regulations gives individuals a right to cancel any orders placed online and to seek compensation for any losses they incur as a result of the non-compliance. The Office of Fair Trading and the local Trading Standards Office are empowered to enforce the regulations under their existing enforcement regime.

The Electronic Commerce Regulations also operate to regulate the provision of goods and services by UK-based operations trading outside the UK. Service providers located in the UK are required to comply with UK law even if services are provided in another EU member state.

THE ROLE OF PRODUCT PROVIDER

The implications of data protection law are dictated by the role of the organisation in a particular situation. They will differ, for example, between the party that obtains personal information and the party to which that information is subsequently disclosed. They will differ between the party that processes the information for marketing and broking purposes and the party that processes it as a product provider. So it is important to correctly identify the role of the organisation because this impacts on subject information provided to the individual.

The product provider is the organisation that is the ultimate provider of the product or service. In the case of insurance products, it is the insurance company, in the case of bank or building society deposits, it is the bank or building society. More complex examples involve products apparently provided by one organisation but in fact outsourced to a third party; for example, legal expenses insurance is an add-on to many motor or home insurance policies. One particular insurance company has specialised in providing legal expenses cover that involves substantial investment in a telephone assistance scheme. In this example the product provider is the specialist insurance company not the intermediary general insurance companies, although they are product providers for motor and home insurance. Also, legal expenses cover is likely to be a 'block' policy: this is cover for a group of individuals coordinated through either an intermediary or, in the case of legal expenses, another product provider.

The product provider may promote its products directly or, as in the case of a finance house attached to a retailer, may rely on business from interested third parties. Commission is usually paid to an intermediary by the product provider for making a recommendation or because it has an interest in a related transaction, for example, a retail sale on credit. Many product providers accept business direct from consumers as well as maintaining indirect distribution channels.

THE ROLE OF THE INTERMEDIARY

Intermediaries range from independent brokers who provide guidance and advice on a range of financial products and those parties involved in a related transaction (to the financial service) authorised to make recommendations to consumers or product providers. Parties likely to be involved only in making recommendations include estate agents assisting in the advancement of a property sale or solicitors advising on options for separating couples or family trust arrangements.

As with product providers there is a wide range of sizes of intermediary firms, from multinational brokers servicing the insurance requirements of the world's largest companies and largest risks, to small high-street outlets for impartial financial advice to consumers and small businesses. The element they have in common is that they are not the ultimate provider of the product being bought; they may act in every way as the key contact with the customer or client, but the eventual contract is made between product provider and customer. This differs from the situation where a product provider outsources administration to a third party; for example, medical insurance arrangements are often underwritten by one company but administered by another. The product provider remains the contracting party in that example; it is not an intermediary.

The traditional role of the independent intermediary is to seek out the best product terms on behalf of its principal. The intermediary is the agent of the client, not the product provider and is committed to providing independent advice across the entire available market. Some intermediaries offer insurance cover under block policies. The product provider underwrites the block policy for the benefit of an unidentified group of individuals. The intermediary may be aware of the identity of the individuals or not, it may be an employer's insured scheme so that the employer is the only party to have personal data until the individual makes a claim on the policy. At that point, the liaison is conducted via the intermediary, not direct with the product provider.

Polarisation of intermediary roles due to regulation means that many intermediaries are in fact tied agents of a product provider. This is the case with in-house sales representatives, most banks and building societies and those intermediaries who refer business to a product provider without any advice as to the appropriateness of a particular product or the performance and stability of the product provider.

Banks and building societies are some of the most complex organisations in financial services. They are often product providers in the relationship with the customer, for example, where deposits and mortgages are concerned. They may also act as intermediary for other financial products such as investments and insurance. The past 20 years has witnessed a number of banks setting up insurance businesses that remain separate legal entities for regulatory and legal reasons. So even when a referral is made to a company in the same group, the bank is acting as intermediary.

For purposes of providing accurate and complete subject information in advertisements, it is important to identify when prospects are invited to respond direct to the product provider rather than the intermediary. In this case the details required should relate to the product provider, as that is the party that processes the personal data. Similarly, if the intermediary is promoting a product range from a particular product provider, it may be acting as an outsource service supplier to the product provider. This carries data protection implications for the role of the intermediary[10] and its relationship with the product provider. It may also impact on subject information as it will need to include reference to the product provider as well as the intermediary, which may retain ownership of the client for marketing purposes.

AFFINITY MARKETING AND ITS EFFECT ON TRADITIONAL ROLES

Affinity marketing takes place when an organisation seeks to exploit the value of its customer and prospect database by marketing products and services it does not (and possibly cannot) provide itself. A good example is car manufacturers, which often promote a range of branded products provided by third parties under the car manufacturer's brand name. So the affinity marketer is neither a product provider nor is it an intermediary. It positions itself as product provider but in fact is merely fronting the real product provider; somewhere in the small print there will be wording to explain the real identity of the product provider, the party that contracts with the customer.

Data protection law is a key reason behind the development of affinity marketing in the UK. A customer database is a valuable asset that organisations want to exploit; however, data protection law protects the database. Only those customers who have been made aware that their information may be disclosed to third parties for marketing purposes and who have consented to that disclosure, can be approached directly by third parties. To work around this restriction, the database owner may take a more active role in the promotion of the product. It may brand the product as its own and ostensibly promote it to its customers in newsletters, direct mailshots, and so on. The administration of the product is outsourced to the product provider. The respective roles of product provider and affinity marketer vary in practice from both parties actively promoting the product at one end of the spectrum to the affinity marketer offering a 'virtual' product with all aspects of marketing, delivery and administration being outsourced to the product provider.

---

10 See Chapter 10 on the seventh principle.

The effect on traditional roles of product provider and intermediary is minimal. Many prospective affinity marketers approach, or are approached by, an intermediary that plays an active part in setting up the affinity arrangement. At regular intervals, the intermediary approaches the market on behalf of the affinity marketer to negotiate new, hopefully better, terms. In this, the intermediary is performing its traditional function on behalf of its principal.

The effect of affinity marketing carries more profound implications in data protection terms. For purposes of providing accurate and complete subject information in advertisements, it is important to identify the roles of the product provider and the advertiser/database owner. It is critical to the issue of marketing consent that the marketer and the product provider keep very clear lines of responsibility. The initial approach to the prospect must be made by or on behalf of the database owner, who is the party with authority to approach the prospects on the database relying on subject information and marketing clauses.

The advertisement may carry information to allow the relationship to develop in one of two ways. First, the prospect may be invited to respond direct to the product provider, akin to a host mailing. In this case, the subject information statement must explain the relationship and the role of the product provider in processing the prospect's personal data. Alternatively, the fulfilment of the product purchase and subsequent administration may be branded to continue to appear as though the product is being provided by the advertiser/database owner. This latter is a true affinity marketing arrangement. In these circumstances the subject information statement should relate to the advertiser.

Once again, in both host mailing and affinity marketing relationships there are data protection implications for the role of the intermediary,[11] the product provider and the relationship between them.

CONCLUSION

This chapter has considered how far data protection provisions apply to promotions that do not use personal data. These types of advertisement provide a channel of communication with prospects and customers and so provide an opportunity to start communicating the organisation's data protection policies and, given the importance of subject information, it is suggested that appropriate statements be included in most advertisements. It is recognised, however, that certain advertisements are not appropriate vehicles for data protection statements, due to either shortage of space or the advertising medium itself. Product leaflets designed to be picked up by customers

---

11 See Chapter 10 on the seventh principle.

in a branch or sent out in response to a telephone or postal enquiry are an excellent way of communicating data protection policies early in the customer relationship.

The key information that must be supplied to individuals before they provide any personal information to the organisation is known as 'subject information'. As subject information constitutes the organisation's authority to process personal information fairly, it is critical that appropriate messages about the identity of the organisation and the purposes for which it processes personal information are communicated prior to any personal information being obtained. In particular, those advertisements that invite an initial response from the customer that includes providing personal information, notably websites and off-the-page coupons, must include subject information – otherwise subsequent processing of the personal information obtained will not be fair in relation to the first data protection principle.

Another aspect of disclosure of personal information relates to outsourcing and affinity relationships that raise issues of control of the information. This is particularly important when assessing record-keeping requirements, dealt with in later chapters of this book and particularly the outsourcing relationships discussed in Chapter 19. Also, the role of the advertiser impacts on the content of marketing and opt-out clauses. The parties, product provider, intermediary and affinity marketer must resolve issues around ownership of the customer and ensure that subject information is accurate so that consumers know what marketing material to expect from whom in future. In the final analysis, the Information Commissioner will consider the expectations of the consumer based on the data protection policies communicated to them by the parties.

CHAPTER 13

Marketing and Privacy Issues

Many types of advertising use personal information to target prospects. Examples include direct mail, affinity promotions and personalised email and text messaging; all forms of direct marketing. This chapter considers the privacy-related issues surrounding the use of personal information for this type of targeted promotion.

Special rules apply to specific forms of direct marketing, for example the new 'anti-spam' rules that relate to email marketing, or the telecommunications regulations which govern marketing by telephone or facsimile (fax). These special rules are also explored in this chapter.

In cases where the organisation wishes to pass on or sell lists of marketing prospects, the authority to market (based on subject information and a marketing opt-out clause) must include products and services provided by third parties. Where the permission to market is limited to the products and services of the database owner, affinity marketing or host mailing may be options for allowing third parties to approach prospects. These options are examined and the data protection implications of each are considered in this chapter.

DEFINITION OF DIRECT MARKETING

A wide definition of direct marketing was offered by the Federation of European Direct Marketing (a body that represents the direct marketing sector at European level). FEDMA stated:

> *Direct marketing is a collection of methodologies for communicating a message to individuals with a view to obtaining a measurable, cost-effective response. The most important communication channels for direct marketing are direct mail, mail order, door-to-door, tele-services and call centres, direct response TV, radio and posters and the Internet.*[1]

---

1   FEDMA online glossary of terms. Available from www.fedma.org/code/page.cfm?id_page=268#liens04.

The Data Protection Act 1998 (the Act) refers to direct marketing as 'the communication (by whatever means) of any advertising or marketing material which is directed to particular individuals'.[2]

A GENERAL RULE FOR DIRECT MARKETING

The previous chapter considered the implications of providing subject information to meet the requirements of the first data protection principle. In addition to subject information, fair and lawful marketing depends on giving a prospect the opportunity to opt out of receiving direct marketing material and respecting any indication that they want to opt out.

The key criterion before commencing any direct marketing campaign is to check that appropriate subject information and marketing opt-out have been provided to prospects. The organisation is then free to approach any prospect who has not opted out. Special rules then apply to the direct marketing approaches by mail, telephone, fax, text and email that are considered below.

SPECIAL RULES FOR DIRECT MAIL

The rules relating to direct mail primarily involve ensuring accurate and up-to-date personal information on marketing prospects and providing adequate subject information to recipients.

ENSURING MARKETING LISTS ARE ACCURATE AND UP TO DATE

To ensure that personal information used for direct mail is as accurate and up to date as possible, the DMA requires its members to 'clean' mailing lists prior to use. Name and address 'cleaning' includes checking standard abbreviations for titles, and how these are shown on both letter and envelope, and correct decoration suffixes. Common misspellings, omissions and transpositions should also be corrected.

The next step is to 'de-duplicate' the mailing list, which involves matching names and addresses featured on the list to remove duplicate records. De-duplication also involves screening for validation and suppression markers to ensure that unwilling prospects are not targeted. A suppression marker would be in use if a prospect had opted out of the use of their personal information for marketing purposes or if a prospect had exercised the right to prevent the use of their personal information for marketing purposes under the Act.

---

2   Data Protection Act 1998, section 11.

A further check for unwilling prospects is to match the mailing list against the Mailing Preference Service (MPS). This non-profit-making body maintains a list of surnames and addresses of people who want to opt out of receiving marketing material. The *DM Code of Practice*[3] requires advertisers to screen their mailing lists against the MPS list before use and to remove unwilling prospects from an intended mailing. Although use of the MPS is not a legal requirement, many industry codes of practice include a requirement for direct marketers to use the service and mailing lists are normally rented on terms that include being 'cleaned' against the MPS list. It is also a benchmark check that the Information Commissioner would expect direct marketers to undertake.

However, registration with MPS will not automatically suppress direct mailings from organisations that have had dealings with the individual in the past. Where there has been previous contact, the organisation is entitled to make direct marketing approaches from time to time regardless of the MPS suppression list unless and until the individual writes to request that it cease using their personal data for direct marketing.

SPECIAL RULES FOR TELEPHONE CALLING

The sending of unsolicited faxes and making unsolicited telephone calls for purposes of direct marketing have both been regulated since May 1999.[4] The provisions were introduced early due to pressing consumer concerns and continue in force as the Privacy and Electronic Communications (EC Directive) Regulations 2003 (the 'Regulations').

The Regulations regulate the use of publicly available telecommunications services for direct marketing purposes. They apply to a wide range of marketing including promotion of goods or services as well as corporate advertising, the promotion of the organisation's aims and ideals. Enforcement of the Regulations is the responsibility of the Information Commissioner[5] either on his own initiative, or at the request of the Director General of Telecommunications or a person aggrieved by the alleged contravention.

The term 'direct marketing' is not defined in the Regulations but the Information Commissioner states[6] that it covers a wide range of activities, not just the offer for sale of goods or services, 'but also the promotion of an organisation's aims and ideals'.

---

3 *DM Code of Practice*, para. 14.3.
4 Direct Marketing Regulations 1998 now revoked and incorporated within The Privacy and Electronic Communications (EC Directive) 2003.
5 The Information Commissioner is the regulatory authority for Data Protection and Freedom of Information in the UK.
6 Guidance to the Privacy and Electronic Communications (EC Directive) Regulations 2003.

There are three main requirements in the Regulations affecting the use of publicly available telecommunications services for direct marketing purposes. First, there are prohibitions on certain activities; second, there is a duty to provide information when making direct marketing telephone calls or sending faxes for direct marketing purposes; third, they provide for the Fax Preference Service (FPS) and the Telephone Preference Service (TPS).

THE PROHIBITIONS

The Regulations prohibit three main activities relevant to marketing by telephone: the use of automated calling systems for direct marketing purposes, sending unsolicited faxes for direct marketing purposes to parties (corporate entities as well as individuals) that have objected to receiving such faxes, and making unsolicited telephone calls to individual subscribers for purposes of direct marketing.

AUTOMATED CALLING SYSTEMS

An automated calling system is one that is capable of automatically initiating a sequence of calls to more than one destination in accordance with instructions stored in the system. This definition means that automated calling systems are those that dial and relay a recorded message without human intervention. It does not include text, picture or video messages, faxes or email. Nor does it cover automated dialling systems that facilitate live telephone conversations when the subscriber picks up the telephone.

The prohibition, set out in Regulation 19, is on the use of automated calling systems for direct marketing purposes to either individual or corporate subscribers unless previous consent has been obtained. Consent must be indicated by a positive act, and cannot be inferred from silence or inaction, although it could be built into contract terms. Note also that consent must have been given prior to the automated call being made.

THE DIFFERENCE BETWEEN UNSOLICITED AND UNWANTED MATERIAL

The term 'unsolicited' is not defined in the Regulations but the Information Commissioner takes the view that it means uninvited.[7] In general, a prohibition against unsolicited approaches does not apply if the intended recipient has previously consented to such approaches or specifically requested information from the advertiser. Such consent will be effective until it is specifically revoked. Also, the fact that the individual subsequently registers with the TPS will not automatically

---

7   Guidance to the Privacy and Electronic Communications (EC Directive) Regulations 2003 is available on the Information Commissioner's website, www.informationcommissioner.gov.uk.

override their prior consent. This is because the Regulations apply to unsolicited calls, so prior consent makes the call one that has been 'solicited' for these purposes.

That the Regulations only apply to 'unsolicited calls' is key. If a coupon has been completed and returned by fax asking for further information about a product or service and has asked for the information to be sent to a particular fax or telephone number, then a call to that number to provide the information requested is not unsolicited.

UNSOLICITED AND UNWANTED FAXES

By Regulation 20 a fax sent for purposes of direct marketing to an individual is unlawful except where the subscriber has consented to the use of that fax number for direct marketing. Also it is unlawful to send an unsolicited fax to either a corporate entity or an individual if that party has registered with the Fax Preference Service (FPS). The prohibition can be overcome only if the recipient contacts the sender and requests information be sent to them on that fax number.

A higher degree of protection is afforded to individuals, as it is unlawful to send a fax for direct marketing purposes unless specifically requested to do so, whereas a corporate entity must register with FPS to prevent unsolicited faxes from being sent. Note that 'individuals' usually includes sole traders and sole practitioners because they are not corporate entities. It also includes 'an unincorporated body of such individuals' per Regulation 2(1).

UNSOLICITED AND UNWANTED TELEPHONE CALLS

By Regulation 21, making unsolicited telephone calls for purposes of direct marketing to an individual who has previously registered with the TPS is unlawful.

The Privacy and Electronic Communications (EC Directive) (Amendment) Regulations 2004 offer corporate subscribers the same protection as individual subscribers allowing them to register with TPS. It is also unlawful to make an unsolicited telephone call for purposes of direct marketing to an individual who has previously notified the organisation that they do not wish to be contacted. The Information Commissioner highlighted the point that there is no requirement for the individual to exercise this right in writing, so a telephone call or email would suffice to put the organisation on notice that a particular individual did not wish to receive marketing telephone calls from it.[8] Many organisations require consumers to notify them in writing when opting out of direct marketing activity but, given the view of the Information Commissioner, this seems an inflexible approach. Efforts should be made

---

8   Information Commissioner, _Legal Advice – Telecoms Guidance_, para. 6.4.2. Document now withdrawn.

to accommodate face-to-face objections in a branch office and telephone objections where the identity of the caller can reasonably be ascertained and confirmed.

The prohibition can be overcome only if the subscriber has given the caller permission to make a marketing telephone call to that number. The subscriber must give permission prior to the call being made.

THE INFORMATION REQUIREMENTS

The Regulations also set out standards of behaviour when making a telephone call for purposes of direct marketing whether using an automated calling system or not. The information that the caller must give[9] is:

- their name, although if the call is made on behalf of a company, the name of the company is required;

- on request, an address or a freephone number on which the caller can be contacted.

The Regulations apply to faxes sent for purposes of direct marketing. They also must include the caller's name and either their address or a freephone number on which they can be contacted. The 'caller' for these purposes is the organisation at whose instigation the call is made; it is not the individual agent or employee who makes the call. Also if the calls are made by an outbound call service supplier on behalf of an organisation, the responsibility for compliance remains with the organisation at whose instigation the call is made, it is not the responsibility of the outbound call service supplier.

The information required in any case must not be misleading and must be sufficient to enable the recipient of the call to trace the caller subsequently.

THE FAX PREFERENCE SERVICE AND THE TELEPHONE PREFERENCE SERVICE

The Regulations impose an obligation on OFCOM to maintain a record of telephone numbers of individual and corporate subscribers who have registered an objection to receiving unsolicited direct marketing faxes and telephone calls.

The maintenance of the TPS and FPS lists has been outsourced to the DMA. The role of the DMA in this context extends beyond simply maintaining the TPS and FPS lists; it also logs complaints from registered subscribers and makes preliminary enquiries into the circumstances of the complaint with the marketing callers or senders of marketing

---

9   Regulation 24.

faxes. It produces reports of its findings and an outline of cases is supplied to the Information Commissioner on a regular basis.

The TPS allows sole traders and partnerships to register as well as individuals. Since June 2004, corporate subscribers have also been allowed to register their numbers with TPS.[10] Once a party is registered with TPS and their telephone number has been included on the register for more than 28 days, it is unlawful to make an unsolicited direct marketing telephone call to that number.

The FPS allows individuals and corporate bodies to register so that their details may not be used for marketing by fax. As a general rule, it is unlawful to send a direct marketing fax to a named individual without their prior consent. It is also unlawful to send an unsolicited direct marketing fax to an individual or corporate subscriber who has registered with FPS. Likewise, an individual or corporate body may notify the sender of marketing material by fax that they do not wish to receive such faxes. In this case it is unlawful to send a direct marketing fax, as consent has been withdrawn.

SPECIAL RULES FOR MARKETING BY EMAIL AND TEXT MESSAGING

To recap the relevant provisions of the Regulations: there are prohibitions on certain activities and there is a duty to provide information when making direct marketing approaches.

THE REGULATIONS

In broad terms, marketing to consumers using electronic means is subject to two new rules. First, email or text messaging to promote goods or services is prohibited unless it is undertaken with the express consent of the individual.[11] Second, specific information requirements apply to marketing messages sent by electronic means. Note that the Privacy and E-comms Regulations do not apply to emails sent to businesses or to email addresses of individuals at work.

PROHIBITION ON UNSOLICITED MARKETING BY EMAIL OR TEXT

The prohibition on marketing by electronic means without consent means that consumers must 'opt in' to receive marketing emails or text messages; this sets a higher standard than for direct marketing generally, which gives the consumer the opportunity to 'opt out' of receiving targeted marketing material. In practical terms, it means that those customers who have not opted out of direct marketing previously

---

10 Privacy and Electronic Communications (EC Directive) (Amendment) Regulations 2004 2002/58/EC.
11 This is also a provision of the *British Code of Advertising Practice*, para. 43.3.

must be contacted again for permission to use their email address for marketing or to text advertisements to a mobile telephone. It also means that advertisers must maintain at least two indicators on prospect databases. One indicator signals agreement to direct mail, a second indicator signals a higher level of consent to email or text messaging.

In its consultation document on best practice for marketing by email, the DMA suggests that existing customer and prospect databases be split into three groups:

1. customers and prospects that have provided explicit consent to be communicated with by email and who have not subsequently revoked that consent;

2. existing customers whose email address was obtained in the course of a sale with appropriate notification to the individual that the user would like to send direct marketing emails (this is the 'soft opt-in' explained below);

3. other prospects.

Under the Privacy and E-comms Regulations, only those in groups 1 and 2 may be sent marketing email.

THE 'SOFT OPT-IN'

There is an exception to the prohibition on email marketing and text messaging where existing customers are being offered substantially the same products or services they purchased from the advertiser previously. This is the so-called 'soft opt-in'.

The definition of what is 'substantially the same' has yet to be tested in the Courts, but it can be seen that this is a narrow exception. In guidance,[12] the Information Commissioner said that similar products and services were those that customers would reasonably expect to receive details of from the advertiser.

To meet the criteria of offering products or services which are substantially the same, the DMA is advising its members to ensure that a sale or 'significant' negotiation of a sale has taken place within the last year and that the products or services promoted will be considered similar as judged by the reasonable expectations of the individuals receiving the emails.[13]

---

12 Information Commissioner (2004) *Electronic Communications Guidance*. London: Data Protection Registrar.

13 *Email Marketing Council, Best Practice Guidelines*, para. 2.1.1.

THE INFORMATION REQUIREMENTS OF THE REGULATIONS

A key provision of the Regulations is that an 'unsubscribe' option must be included to give consumers an easy route to notify the sender that they no longer wish to receive marketing material. The unsubscribe option requires a valid address, which could be an email address, a website address or PO box number. There has already been guidance[14] to the effect that a premium rate telephone number to notify a wish to unsubscribe is in contravention of the regulations as its cost means that it is not an 'easy' option.

For text messaging, the use of short codes can constitute a valid address provided the sender ensures that they clearly identify themselves in the message. The use of the short code must not incur a premium rate charge. In guidance,[15] the Information Commissioner suggested the following format for an unsubscribe option for marketing by text messaging: 'XLtd2stopmsgstxt'stop'to(then add 5 digit short code)'.

The DMA recommends a data hygiene policy to 'reduce incorrect, incomplete or outdated addresses, to process online unsubscribe requests immediately, to process suppression requests offline within 10 working days, to inform those opting out how long it will take to be effective'.[16]

In its consultation document[17] on email marketing best practice, the DMA points out that the collection of email addresses from websites, emails and other public domain sources is likely to involve contravention of the Act. Given the requirement for consent to marketing by means of email, it would also breach the Privacy and E-comms Regulations to use email addresses collected from the Internet or otherwise in the public domain for marketing purposes.

A direct marketing email must also feature a clear indication that it is an advertisement. The email must state prominently, preferably in the heading, that it contains marketing material. An example of how to indicate that an email carries an advertising feature would be to use the words 'Advertising feature' or 'Unsolicited commercial communication' either in the subject line of the email or at the top of the body text. The intention is that recipients should be aware that it is a marketing email without having to open it. The email heading must not mask or misrepresent the identity of the sender or the subject matter of the email. Other information requirements are clear contact details, address and telephone number of the sender. Promotional offers must be identified, including terms and conditions and

---

14 *Electronic Communications Guidance.*
15 *Electronic Communications Guidance.*
16 *E-mail Marketing Council, Best Practice Guidelines*, para. 2.2.
17 *E-mail Marketing Council, Best Practice Guidelines*, para. 2.1.

competitions and games must be clearly identified and include their terms and conditions.

The DMA suggests as a guide that emails should not exceed 60 KB in total file size.

The Advertising Standards Authority (ASA) has already made rulings under the Regulations. The first was against a business that failed to clearly indicate that its email contained advertising material and it had not obtained prior consent from those consumers to whom it sent the emails. In another case, the ASA found that prior consent had not been obtained from the recipients of advertising emails sent by a well-known computer company.

The ASA has the power to prevent organisations from advertising if they refuse to change the content of an offending advertisement. Offences can also be pursued by the Information Commissioner and carry a maximum £5000 fine.

A SAMPLE MARKETING EMAIL

An example of wording to meet subject information requirements might be:

> **Advertising feature**
>
> *Text of advertisement.*
>
> *We [XYZ Limited] use name and contact details to tell you about our products and services. We will not pass your details on to any other party but we maintain an active marketing list and we will retain contact details for our historical records. If you wish to unsubscribe to this marketing activity, please click the 'unsubscribe' option below.*
>
> *Street number and name, county and post code. Telephone contact details.*

RENTING OR USING LISTS

When targeting prospective customers whose personal information is held by other organisations, the same legal considerations apply but the implementation of the legal requirements varies. As with own customer marketing lists, adequate and complete subject information statements and valid marketing opt-out (or opt-in for email and text messaging) authority is required before making a direct marketing approach. Marketers must check that prospect lists are data protection compliant before they are obtained. When renting or buying a list, it is appropriate to seek warranties from the list owner that target customers have been advised that their details will be used to market them with goods or services offered by third parties.

These requirements also apply to prospect data sharing within a marketing group. An organisation may choose to present itself as a marketing group, using the same brands and logos as sister or associate companies. However, data protection law does not recognise marketing groups; the focus is on individual corporate entities. As these are separate, so data protection law treats them as completely independent of one another. In consequence, use of personal information on a prospect database owned by a sister company has to be treated in the same way as a mailing list bought in from an external supplier. The advertiser must check that appropriate subject information has been provided, explaining that personal details will be used to market goods or services provided by, in this case, other group companies, and that individuals have been given the opportunity to opt out of that marketing activity.

The use of emailing lists is subject to complex rules under the Privacy and E-comms Regulations. If the intention is to rent a list for marketing by email, the only acceptable practice is to advertise by way of a 'host mailing', that is, one where the database owner introduces marketing material from the advertiser (who is a third party). The database owner undertakes the promotion without disclosing personal information on the prospect database to the advertiser at any time. The database owner must have the express consent of prospects to receiving marketing material by email. In a host mailing, the prospect data is not passed to the marketer unless the database is to be de-duplicated. In that case, use of the data is restricted to de-duplication activity. Outgoing emails should feature the name of the database owner in the 'from' field and the DMA recommends that the name of the advertiser should also appear prominently, either in the 'from' field or in the subject line.

As a minimum, the DMA suggests that the marketer needs to know:

- how and when the list was built;

- what subject information statements or privacy policies were presented at the point of data collection;

- what prospects indicated as to their preferences in respect of future email marketing directed to them;

- how unsubscribe requests have been processed and relevant addresses suppressed;

- whether the database owner is otherwise legally compliant as regards the collection and subsequent use of email addresses.

USING PERSONAL INFORMATION AS MARKETING MATERIAL

PHOTOGRAPHS

A photograph of a recognisable, living, individual is personal information relating to that individual. Before the photograph is taken, the subject information requirements should be met. This means advising the individual concerned of:

- the identity of the organisation that will control the use of the photograph;

- the purposes for which the photograph will be used;

- any other information relevant in the circumstances.

In a case that was not reported officially, a photograph of a disabled child was taken originally to promote a youth centre. It was subsequently used on a poster promoting AIDS awareness. The organisation, in this case a local authority, was found guilty of a breach of the first data protection principle, to process personal information fairly and to provide subject information as specified. Its processing of personal data relating to the child was unfair, as the subject information requirements had not been met.

Recent cases concerning the privacy of celebrities have confirmed the view that a photograph is personal information. In the case involving Naomi Campbell,[18] it was held that, although the model is a celebrity and courts publicity, nevertheless she has a right to privacy in certain areas, particularly where health and medical treatment are concerned. The European Court of Justice has gone even further in a case involving Princess Caroline of Monaco and found that she had a right to privacy when out in public with members of her family as part of her private life.[19]

Models and actors whose photographs are used to promote goods and services are protected by copyright and/or contract law, as are celebrities who use their fame to endorse products for a fee. The protection can be significant: in a recent US case,[20] Nescafé has had to pay its former model substantial damages for using a 20-year-old photograph as a tiny cameo on its coffee jars without paying any royalties. The award, made under a California statute, was for $15.6 million.

---

18 *Campbell* v. *MGN Limited* [2004] UKHL 22.
19 *von Hanover* v. *Germany* [2004] Application no. 59320/00. Judgement from Strasbourg 24 June 2004.
20 Reported in *The Times* Wednesday 2 February 2005, p. 35.

USING CASE STUDIES

Case studies where the facts are based on real persons constitute a use of personal information. As such, the first data protection principle applies requiring processing to be fair and lawful. In particular, the first principle requires that the individuals involved should be given appropriate subject information about the identity of the organisation, the purposes for which their personal history will be processed and any other information relevant in the circumstances. An ordinary statement about the use of information for marketing purposes will not adequately explain the use of that information in case studies. The standard phrase about using personal information for marketing purposes would not lead anyone to believe that any more than their name and contact details and possibly some classifications for profiling purposes will be required. Case studies obviously involve the use of significant amounts of personal information and the purpose of the processing is not to market to the data subject, but to promote products to a wide range of other people. The personal history of the subject of the case study will be disclosed potentially to the general public. If it is intended to use personal information in this way, subject information needs to be very specific and advertisers would be advised to obtain the consent of the individual in writing, for the record.

The Information Commissioner's report for the year ended 31 March 2003 included a reported example of a breach of data protection law in circumstances involving a case study.

> *An employer was setting up procedures for in-house training of its customer-facing staff. To help in this, they needed to find an example upon which to base their new procedures. The example used was of an existing staff member who had recently had occasion to use the company's facilities as a customer. The staff member was unaware that this had taken place, and only realised what had happened when other employees began referring to his experience. The employee requested that the Information Commissioner make an assessment. He assessed that the employer was unlikely to have complied with the Act and recommended appropriate changes to the procedures involved. The employer removed the individual's data and replaced it with a theoretical example not linked to any actual person. They also put in place procedures to safeguard future use of real-world data in their training.[21]*

---

21 Information Commissioner (2003) 'Case Study – Breach: Unfair Processing' *Annual Report and Account,* p. 15. Available from www.informationcommissioner.gov.uk.

The case underlines the dangers of using real-life case studies. Organisations have two options: either obtain the informed consent of the data subject or use fictitious scenarios involving common elements of real-life events.

PUBLISHING INFORMATION ON A WEBSITE

There is an additional concern if the intention is to publish personal information on a website. As information on a website is available to be viewed and downloaded anywhere in the world, the publication of information on a website is deemed to be a transfer of that information outside the member states of the EU. The transfer of personal data outside the EU is a restricted activity under data protection law.[22]

Although there are a number of exceptions to the restriction, it is suggested that the most appropriate authority would be to seek the consent of the individual concerned. Their consent would be required in any event to publish the information at all, so the intention to publish the information on the website should also be explained together with a warning that some third countries may not offer the same level of protection for personal data within their boundaries.

CONCLUSION

Using personal information to target individual prospects or customers is a highly regulated activity. In this chapter, consideration has been given to the wider privacy protection measures in various regulations governing the use of telephone, fax, email and text messaging.

It is important to note that there is no longer one standard authority for direct marketing. Different communication channels and different intended recipients are subject to different rules. Some direct marketing activity is prohibited, such as sending faxes to individuals or corporate entities that have signed up to the FPS. Some direct marketing activities require an opt-in, for example email marketing to individuals and telephone marketing. Other activities require that the intended recipient has the opportunity to opt out, such as direct mail. There is a significant compliance burden to interpreting and applying the relevant law. Marketing personnel should be made aware of this and be encouraged to allow time for compliance personnel to do their job properly. Equally, compliance personnel should be aware of the time pressures relating to the production of advertisements and product literature and be encouraged to be sensitive to the needs of their marketing colleagues. A little cross-training to introduce each to the constraints within which the other works can be invaluable.

---

22 See Chapter 11 on the eighth data protection principle.

There is a key difference between unsolicited and unwanted marketing approaches. An unsolicited approach is one that has not been invited either specifically by consent or indirectly by taking other products or services from the advertiser. Unsolicited approaches are strictly regulated and even prohibited in some circumstances; for example, unsolicited direct marketing approaches by fax to individuals or corporate entities.

Unwanted marketing approaches can be dealt with by the recipient who has recourse to request that the advertiser cease to use their address, telephone number or email address for direct marketing activity. The FPS and TPS also allow individuals and corporate entities to register their objection to receiving unwanted approaches. The MPS is only open to individuals. Failure to observe these preferences may result in regulatory investigation. Note, however, that the preference services do not override specific consent to a marketing approach from an organisation, particularly where goods and services have been supplied previously. Such consent remains in force until specifically revoked. All parties should be aware of the distinction between unwanted and unsolicited material and marketing databases should be structured so as to record the different levels of consent to the use of personal information for purposes of direct marketing.

The brunt of the restrictions on marketing by email falls upon those organisations that market to consumers. The Privacy and E-comms Regulations do not prohibit the use of work email addresses, even to market non-work-related products and services. However, the *British Code of Advertising, Sales Promotion and Direct Marketing* is relevant.[23] It states that unsolicited commercial emails should only be sent to directors and employees of limited companies if they are advertising goods or services relevant to their business activity.

When approaching prospects on marketing lists owned by third parties, the key problem is establishing due authority to allow a third party to approach a prospect on a marketing database unless it was established with this objective and subject information and appropriate marketing opt-outs given. The ways in which an advertiser might still promote goods or services to prospects on a third-party database without due authority were also considered. The third party in these circumstances might be a sister company in a group of companies or might be an external organisation.

When using personal information as marketing content, there are also privacy issues to consider. The use of photographs in which an individual can be identified is already highly regulated by contractual provisions, requiring royalties to be paid to

---

23 *British Code of Advertising,* para. 43.4.

models. Data protection law can add little to this area, although it is worth noting that a photograph is regarded as personal information. Companies must ensure that the photograph is used with the full knowledge of the data subject. Even then, providing adequate subject information before starting to process personal data provides authority to process only as described. Organisations should ensure that subject information is adequate and complete otherwise a breach of the first data protection principle may occur.

Organisations should ensure that they seek the consent of individuals for the use of their personal information for marketing purposes. Where this involves using details as case study material, consent should be based on explicit information about the proposed use of their personal information.

CHAPTER 14

The Sales Process and the Third Principle

The application or enquiry form (real or virtual) is often the first point at which a significant amount of personal information is sought from a prospective customer and therefore the point at which significant data protection implications for creating and holding records arise. There are some implications, too, where the organisation carries out further checks and referrals in respect of the application, for example medical testing, money laundering checks and credit reference checks.

THE ENQUIRY OR APPLICATION FORM

At some point in the sale process the prospect is invited to complete an application form, either in writing, online or by answering questions face to face or on the telephone. Given what has been covered so far in relation to the need for subject information, it is immediately clear that any request for personal information gives rise to the statutory duty to provide subject information. The subject information requirements have been considered in Chapter 5 and the practical implications covered in Chapter 13.

RECORD-KEEPING REQUIREMENTS

At the time of receiving an application, record-keeping requirements start to impact on the sale process. Significant customer records are created that are almost certainly subject to data protection law. Any and all computerised records are automatically subject to data protection; in addition certain paper files are also covered. These are paper records created with the intention of transferring the data to computer at some time in the future and those that are filed in a 'relevant filing system'.

Following the landmark decision in *Durant* v. *Financial Services Authority* [2003],[1] a relevant filing system is one that allows easy identification of files relating to an individual; for example, files held in named, alphabetical order, or by customer number where the customer number can easily be cross-referenced. Files held in date order are unlikely to be in a 'relevant filing system'; however, it is an issue that is

---

1   See Chapter 3 'Definitions'.

decided on the facts. A very disorganised filing system that has deteriorated from named, alphabetical order may not be a relevant filing system if, in practice, it does not allow files relating to specific individuals to be located easily.

Assuming that the records created on receipt of an application form are subject to data protection law, the record-keeping requirements are set out in the data protection principles. In this chapter, the focus is on the third principle, the requirement for personal information to be adequate, relevant and not excessive for the purpose for which it is held and processed.

When designing questionnaires and application forms, what is adequate, relevant and not excessive must be addressed before any personal information is obtained. A key point to note is that the test of what is adequate, relevant and not excessive is carried out in relation to the stated purposes for which the information will be processed. The requirement to provide subject information includes stating these purposes and subsequent processing must be in accordance with subject information. Notably this cannot include previously unidentified and undefined purposes.[2]

The adequacy of information held and its relevance can be assessed jointly. The organisation is creating a customer record of a transaction; full details of the transaction are relevant together with contact details relating to the customer or client. If the organisation is unable to fulfil any of its obligations due to incomplete records, it will be in breach of the fourth data protection principle, the requirement to hold adequate information. The relevance of information may change over time; for example, what is relevant for an existing customer may be less so in relation to a former customer who has closed all of their accounts.

CREATING AND MAINTAINING ADEQUATE RECORDS

The maintenance of adequate records can be achieved and monitored through frequent review of forms and other methods used for collecting information about individuals. Product specifications may change over time, requiring standard forms to be tailored. Also feedback from administrators within the organisation may indicate that wording on forms elicits the wrong responses, again requiring amendment of the wording. Amendment and restructuring of questionnaires, application forms and spoken scripts for call centres should aim to ensure that correctly completed data entry fields provide the right amount and type of information.

Where personal information is obtained from a source other than the subject of the information, the organisation should consider whether it is reasonable to rely on

2   *The Data Protection Principles*, Guideline 4.

information received from that source and whether there are any steps that may be taken to verify the information.

Data entry systems and procedures need to be checked periodically to ensure that they do not themselves allow for the introduction of inaccuracies into the data. A system for rectifying inaccurate data quickly and passing on the corrections to any third parties who might have been allowed access to it is important to demonstrate a compliant position.

The DMA addresses some of the logistical issues that can lead to problems in creating adequate records. It recommends[3] that a coupon in a newspaper or magazine allow sufficient space for all the data elements required. The average UK name and address record is 48 keystrokes long but can involve up to nine separate pieces of information. Clarity is also important if the transcription of information from coupon to computer database is to be carried out efficiently and accurately. The use of blocks or 'tiger teeth' to denominate spacing for characters may help to improve legibility. The DMA suggests that allowance be made for variations in handwriting and ink colour. To help ensure that information provided is complete, specific prompts are recommended for postcode, house number and name. Finally, the DMA recommends that coupons are tested by a friend or colleague prior to sign off.

Data capture over the telephone allows operators to revisit for missing or misheard details and calls can be recorded for later extraction of relevant data. As an operator records information provided by a caller on the telephone, the DMA recommends on-screen prompts for name and address elements, including double checks on key elements such as the postcode. Use should be made of automated validation software such as the Royal Mail software[4] that returns the correct postal address from the postcode entered.

There are also key events in the relationship with the customer that may affect the adequacy and relevance of personal information relating to them. When a prospective customer decides to enter into a contract with the organisation for a particular product or service, the information requirements will automatically increase. The records that were adequate for a prospect need to be supplemented to ensure that all the relevant information is held for a customer.

---

3   Direct Marketing Association (2004) *Best Practice Guidelines – Data in Direct Marketing.* Available from www.dma.org.uk/DocFrame/DocView.asp?id=225&sec=-1.
4   Postcode Address File, available from www.royalmail.com.

CHECKS AND REFERRALS

Applications for financial services usually involve some checking of the credentials of the applicant. An application for credit will be processed by undertaking a credit reference check and may also involve verification of salary and bank details. Applications for deposit and investment accounts are subject to money laundering prevention procedures involving verification of identity and confirmation of contact details. An application for life insurance requires underwriting and that may involve medical questionnaires or medical examinations.

CREDIT APPLICATIONS

The Banking Code provides that financial institutions should assess the customer's ability to repay any borrowing before lending money or increasing overdrafts, credit card limits or other borrowing.[5] *The Banking Code* states that this assessment may include consideration of information from credit reference agencies. It is standard to carry out a credit reference check in respect of the applicant for an application for credit.

In relation to credit referencing, there are three main areas of concern from the data protection perspective. First, the integrity of the credit reference database relies on a two-way flow of information, to and from the lender. So, organisations that utilise credit reference facilities are contracted to supply information about an individual's borrowing and the state of their account. This constitutes a disclosure of personal information relating to the borrower.

Second, credit reference enquiries are made against a household address. This involves the disclosure of personal information relating to other individuals resident at that address. This has led to many complaints to the Information Commissioner over the years and is now the subject of a new procedure in the credit reference industry.

Third, information held by credit reference agencies may be inaccurate or misleading. Consumers are often at a loss to know how to correct the information and it is an area where they may be disadvantaged by the inaccuracies. This means that it is a high-risk area in terms of data protection compliance; any inaccuracies are likely to have a significant effect on the individual concerned and public awareness of credit reference information and its potential impact is high.

---

5   Banking Code Standards Board (2005) *The Banking Code*, para. 13.1. London: British Bankers' Association.

DISCLOSING PERSONAL INFORMATION TO CREDIT REFERENCE AGENCIES

Information held about individuals on credit reference files includes:

- Publicly available records such as the electoral roll, records of County Court judgments and bankruptcies, individual voluntary arrangements and repossession orders.

- Information provided by other lenders about borrowers. This might include information about whether payments have been kept up to date in the past and the current state of existing loans. There is a distinction between so called 'white data' and 'black data'. White data is information about accounts that are up to date and without payment problems. Black data relates to accounts that are in arrears or where there are payment problems.

- A record of credit checks carried out by lenders in the past. This shows the history of the individual's search for credit, so a large number of applications made over a short period of time could be seen as an indication of over-commitment or even fraud.

The key data protection issue is that lenders are contractually bound to the credit agency to share with it personal information about the state of an individual's account from time to time. This disclosure must be authorised by reference to the lender's notification entry (the entry on the data protection register), showing credit agencies as a disclosure for information processed in relation to loan administration. It must also be authorised by reference to subject information given to the individuals to whom the personal information relates. Subject information is required pursuant to the first data protection principle, the duty to inform individuals of the identity of the organisation, the purposes for which personal information will be processed and any other information relevant in the circumstances. What is relevant in the circumstances includes relevant disclosures. Sharing account information with a credit reference agency would be a relevant disclosure.

The Banking Code distinguishes between 'white' and 'black' data relating to a customer loan account. Paragraph 13.6 provides that information about personal debts may be disclosed to credit reference agencies if:

- the customer has fallen behind with repayments;

- the amount owed is not in dispute;

- the customer has failed to make satisfactory proposals for repaying the debt, following a formal demand.

However, it is still a data protection requirement to inform customers taking out a debt that their information will be disclosed to the credit reference agency should the above circumstances apply.

On the other hand, paragraph 13.8 refers to the situation regarding white data and provides that information about the day-to-day running of an account may be disclosed to a credit reference agency only if the customer has consented to the disclosure.

INFORMATION RELATING TO THIRD PARTIES

In privacy terms, there is a problem relating to the information extracted from the credit reference agency's database in response to an enquiry from a lender. Enquiries have traditionally been made against the applicant's address. The information provided in response may include information about persons linked to the address searched, other than the individual who is seeking credit and who is the subject of the inquiry. This has led to notable cases in the Data Protection Tribunal.[6] The position is impossible to defend in many ways. A credit reference enquiry could elicit personal information without the consent or even knowledge of the persons concerned relating to:

- other family members with the same name;

- other family members who are financially dependent on the applicant;

- previous residents at the stated address.

Since the autumn of 2004, a new protocol has been in place which credit reference agencies have adopted. The new regime provides:

- There will no longer be an assumption made that there is a financial connection simply on the basis of a shared surname and address. This recognises that parents and children should not be automatically assumed to be financially connected.

- When customers request access to their credit file, the process will be amended so that an individual will only see their own credit data and not that of any financially connected third party.

- Individuals will be able to opt out of the automatic use of their financial partner's data enabling them to be assessed in their own right.

- An 'alert process' using household information will be created, providing lenders with the ability to detect fraud.

---

6   *Equifax Europe Limited* v. *The Data Protection Registrar* [1991] DA/90/25/49/7. *CCN Systems Limited* v. *CCN Credit Systems Limited* [1991] DA/90/25/49/9.

INACCURATE INFORMATION

This is largely an issue for the credit reference agencies. However, the impact of relying on inaccurate information supplied by a credit reference agency might result in an individual being denied credit and potentially suffering a pecuniary loss as a result, either through a missed opportunity or by obtaining credit elsewhere on less advantageous terms. A key factor that the Information Commissioner considers when assessing a complaint is the steps taken by the organisation whose records are incorrect to inform third parties who may be relying on the inaccurate information.

AUTOMATED DECISION TAKING

During the application process, it is not uncommon for certain decisions to be taken by automated means. Credit scoring software and insurance underwriting systems are routinely used. Personal information relating to the applicant is entered into the system and the software makes a preliminary decision whether or not the applicant meets the basic criteria for the application to be pursued to the next stage. Automated systems are a useful tool, allowing semi-skilled operators to process applications on the basis of sophisticated underwriting or other selection criteria. They help to reduce operating costs and reduce the waiting time for decisions to be made.

The Data Protection Act 1998 (the Act) gives individuals the right to challenge decisions made by purely automated means. The decision must have a significant and adverse effect on the individual or another living person and there are qualifying conditions such as the requirement that the objection must be made in writing.[7]

On receipt of an objection to a decision made by automated means, the organisation is obliged to review the personal information supplied and the decision reached. The review must be carried out by an individual rather than by the system and there is no pressure to find in favour of either party. The simple intervention of a human being in the decision-making process is sufficient to meet the requirements of the Act and answer the exercise of the right to object to decisions made by automated means.

MONEY LAUNDERING PREVENTION MEASURES

There are two main aspects to money laundering prevention measures. First, the 'know your customer' regime, which dictates that financial institutions verify the identity of their customers, and second, the subsequent monitoring of activity on the customer's account for unusual transactions and activity that might indicate a money laundering issue.

---

7   See Chapter 9 on the sixth data protection principle.

'KNOW YOUR CUSTOMER'

Under the Money Laundering Regulations 2003, all banks, building societies and other providers of financial services have had to put procedures in place to prevent money laundering. The procedures, as developed by the Joint Money Laundering Steering Group, require institutions to verify a potential customer's identity and address, using separate checks.[8] More checks are needed in the case of account opening where the customer is not physically present as, for example, with telephone and Internet banking.

'Know your customer' involves obtaining personal information for purposes of money laundering prevention measures. To meet the subject information requirements of the first principle, the purposes for which the information is required should be explained to customers. An FSA consultation paper, *Reducing Money Laundering Risk – Know Your Customer and Anti-Money Laundering Monitoring* makes the point that the FSA does '… not consider that data protection considerations constrain the effective use by firms of KYC ['know your customer'] information to meet legal or regulatory requirements'.[9]

This is an accurate statement so long as the data protection implications are taken into account early in the transaction and dealt with appropriately. We have already considered the issues relating to subject information.[10] The key to compliance with subject information requirements is to identify all intended processing activity in advance of obtaining any personal information. Then, at the point of data capture, the individual supplying the information can be given a complete and accurate statement of the processing activity of the organisation and any other information relevant in the circumstances.

The record-keeping requirements are set out in the data protection principles and require that personal information be accurate and kept up to date where necessary. The information held must be adequate, relevant but not excessive for the purpose and records must be held securely. 'Know your customer' relies on individual customers providing specified documents to prove their identity and, separately, their address. *The Banking Code* notes that not all customers will have access to documentation that would appear on the standard list of acceptable documents to establish identity or address, and it suggests that subscribers be flexible in their approach to such customers. It is suggested that the customer should be asked what evidence of their identity or address they can produce, with a senior official of the institution prepared and trained to make a decision as to the acceptability of the evidence that the customer

---

8   The Money Laundering Regulations 2003 SI No. 3075.
9   Financial Services Authority (2003) *Reducing Money Laundering Risk – Know Your Customer and Anti-Money Laundering Monitoring* DP22. Available from www.fsa.gov.uk.
10 Chapter 12 on advertising.

can provide. What is relevant and adequate to the financial institution depends on it being able to satisfy the anti-money laundering requirements of the 'know your customer' regime; however, in any one particular case it may be excessive to demand production of those specified documents if, for any reason, a customer is unable to provide them.

If inaccurate information is held concerning a customer transaction and that forms the basis of a referral to relevant authorities as a potential money laundering involvement, there could be serious ramifications for the customer. This is likely to be a sensitive area and customers will be aggrieved at the intrusion if it is found to be based on inaccurate or incomplete information. Compensation may be claimed by individuals through the courts if their data protection rights are breached and they suffer loss or damage as a result. A key factor that the Information Commissioner takes into account when assessing a complaint is the impact on the individual concerned of the inaccuracy of the information.

ANTI-MONEY LAUNDERING MONITORING

A good definition of anti-money laundering monitoring is provided by FSA in its consultation document, *Reducing Money Laundering Risk*, which states that anti-money laundering monitoring is:

> *a firm's use of systems and controls to be actively alert to indications of unusual use by a customer of its products and services. And through this to seek to detect and address circumstances that suggest that their products and services may be being used to launder money.*[11]

This describes the use of systems and controls outside normal product and service administration; certainly the processing is not being undertaken for the benefit of the individual client, rather for the common good of all. Therefore the processing of personal information as part of those systems and controls will fall outside of the reasonable expectations of the individual customer. Initially, therefore, there is an additional processing purpose for disclosure in subject information provided to potential clients at the start of the relationship.

There is a further data protection implication in relation to anti-money laundering initiatives involving the disclosure of personal information by an organisation to the regulatory authority if a particular client or transaction by a client is suspect.

The disclosure of personal information by a money laundering reporting officer is a disclosure that is required by law; it is a provision of the Money Laundering

---

11 *Reducing Money Laundering Risk*, para. 4.2.

Regulations 2001. The Act provides an exemption for disclosures for the purposes of prevention or detection of crime and the apprehension or prosecution of offenders.[12] As such, the disclosure of information about an individual suspected of money laundering is authorised without reference to what that individual might expect or condone. The safeguard for the privacy of individuals relies on the organisation following its internal procedures and making the disclosure via its appointed money laundering reporting officer. So long as procedures are followed, it is unlikely that the Information Commissioner would challenge a disclosure purporting to be made under the exemption outlined. However, if procedures are not observed, a disclosure might be seen as indicative of a systemic problem within the organisation.

MEDICAL REPORTS

In certain circumstances, a life insurance company may require a customer to undergo a medical examination. This might include circumstances where more specific medical testing is considered appropriate, such as genetic testing for hereditary diseases. The most common circumstance is where a significant sum insured would become payable on the death of an applicant for life insurance. Other circumstances where a medical might be required would be in claims management, to establish a claim or to ascertain the degree of disability to which the claimant is subject. All information relating to the physical or mental health of a living individual is classified as 'sensitive data' under the Act and there are tighter controls over processing such information. The issues relating to sensitive data are considered in the next chapter.

GENETIC TESTING

When handling personal information comprising the results of genetic tests, member organisations of the Association of British Insurers (ABI) must adhere to the *Genetic Testing – ABI Code of Practice*.[13] A specialist committee rules on which genetic tests are sufficiently reliable to be taken into account in underwriting a life insurance proposal and the *Genetic Testing* code of practice regulates how the results may be used. There is currently a moratorium on the use of genetic tests in medical underwriting, which means that applicants cannot be asked to undergo a genetic test although it may use the results of genetic tests provided by the applicant in some circumstances.

There is an exception to the moratorium in the case of Huntingdon's disease; an underwriter can ask whether a person making a proposal for life insurance has had a genetic test for Huntingdon's disease. In addition, a person applying for life insurance

---

12 The Data Protection Act 1998, section 29 (1) (a) and (b).
13 Association of British Insurers (1999) *Genetic Testing – ABI Code of Practice* (2nd edition). Available from www.abi.org.uk.

might choose to reveal the results of genetic tests to overcome a presumption in the case of a family history of a particular disease or illness. It is believed that the current moratorium will continue in place for the foreseeable future.

Key points of the Genetic Testing – ABI Code of Practice

This is a summary of the key points in the *Genetic Testing – ABI Code of Practice*:

- An individual cannot be asked to undergo a genetic test.

- If an individual discloses the results of a genetic test and the underwriter wishes to take it into account, they must consult a medical practitioner, usually the insurance company's chief medical officer, before making a decision.

- The prior explicit consent of the individual is required for the use of the results of a genetic test for underwriting purposes. The underwriter must fully specify the purposes for which the information will be applied and any disclosure of the information to third parties.

- The results of a genetic test may not be taken into account for preferred life underwriting, that is, to offer an individual lower rates of insurance than the average based on a clear genetic test. The results of a genetic test may only be applied to reduce a potential loading due to family history.

- The results of a genetic test disclosed by one individual may not be linked with, or otherwise taken into account, when assessing an application from another person such as a blood relation.

- Underwriters are not allowed to ask an individual for the results of genetic tests undergone by another person, such as a blood relation.

- Underwriting organisations are required to monitor to ensure that their staff comply with the *Genetic Testing – ABI Code of Practice*.

- Organisations must respect the confidentiality of genetic test results and take steps to ensure their security. In particular:

  - The organisation must restrict access to the results of genetic tests to those staff who need to know in order to do their job.

  - The results of genetic tests are not to be disclosed to any third parties without the individual's prior explicit, informed consent.

The *Genetic Testing – ABI Code of Practice* was developed with advice and guidance from the Information Commissioner. There is no direct guidance from the Information Commissioner on genetic testing in relation to insurance underwriting;

however, there has been guidance published on the use of genetic testing in relation to human resources management.

In relation to HR management, it is accepted that genetic testing is sometimes valid on health and safety grounds in exceptional circumstances. Guidance from the Information Commissioner, to be found in the *Employment Code*,[14] suggests appropriate benchmarks when using genetic testing in relation to employees. Suggested procedures are based on the conclusions of the Human Genetics Advisory Commission, which has examined the implications of genetic testing.

The *Employment Code*, while not directly applicable to medical underwriting, nevertheless gives an indication of the type of safeguard the Information Commissioner would expect when organisations are dealing with genetic testing.

The general strategies to facilitate compliance with data protection requirements when obtaining medical reports are simply to keep the individual concerned fully informed as to what information will be required and what medical tests, if any, may be required. Processing of the sensitive data relating to health in these circumstances must be authorised by the consent of the individual. Such consent must be informed and specific to the purposes for which it will be used.

CONCLUSION

As the sale process involves collecting and processing a significant volume of personal information, so the record-keeping implications become more significant and require greater effort for compliance. Customer or client records may contain confidential or sensitive information that could cause damage and distress if it were to be revealed publicly. Likewise errors in data recording could have significant ramifications and consumers have the right to pursue organisations for compensation if they are disadvantaged by processing of their personal information that is not compliant with data protection law.

The specific issues relating to the creation of prospect and customer records relate to how information is obtained and managed. The key to compliance is for an intelligent assessment to be made initially of the likely information requirements of a particular product or service and for questionnaires and data gathering gateways to be designed to meet the requirements identified. Regular checks are to key to ensuring that systemic problems do not arise and continue unaddressed.

---

14 Employment Code, section 4.5, 'Workers' Health'.

CHAPTER 15

Using Sensitive Data

SENSITIVE CATEGORIES OF INFORMATION

The Data Protection Act 1998 (the Act) specifies categories of personal information that are defined as 'sensitive data'. The categories are taken directly from the EC Directive on which the UK data protection law is based.[1] These are:

- details of race or ethnic origin
- information relating to an individual's physical or mental health
- information relating to an individual's sexual life
- details of criminal convictions, allegations of criminal offences, court proceedings for any offence
- information about religious or philosophical beliefs
- details of trade union membership
- information about political beliefs.

Applications for many financial services require information from one or more of these sensitive categories of data; for example, life insurance underwriting requires details of the health of the proposer and close blood relations. In addition, details of criminal offences and convictions may be relevant to general insurance; for example, motoring convictions are relevant to motor insurance.

The Act provides that one or more conditions for fair processing be met when processing personal information and that additional conditions for fair processing apply when processing sensitive data. The general fair processing conditions are not covered in this part of the book; they generally apply to legitimate business interests so long as the processing is fair and legal.[2] However, the additional conditions which apply to processing sensitive data are far more restrictive and the focus of this chapter.

---

1   EC Directive 95/46/EC.
2   See Chapter 4 on the first data protection principle for an analysis of the conditions for fair processing personal information generally.

SENSITIVE DATA IN THE APPLICATION PROCESS

The most generally applicable condition is that the individual to whom the information relates has given their explicit consent to the processing of personal information relating to themselves. This would be a logical condition on which to rely when requesting sensitive data from the individual themselves as part of an application process, for example. Then the individual may make a decision whether or not to supply the information requested. If they decline to supply the information, the application process will go no further.

Note that the requirement for fair processing of sensitive categories of data is for 'explicit' consent. There is no definition of 'explicit consent' in the Act, but it is taken to mean an informed and specific affirmation. Consent must be freely given and must constitute an indication that the data subject signifies their agreement; inaction will not suffice. A clear problem with the conditions for fair processing of sensitive data then arises: how to obtain the consent of individuals who are not applying for a product or service but whose personal information is nevertheless required for medical underwriting purposes.

A supplement to the conditions listed in the Act, the Data Protection (Processing of Sensitive Data) Order 2000 (Sensitive Data Order), allows the processing of sensitive data necessary for the purpose of carrying on an insurance business or making determinations in connection with eligibility for, and benefits payable under, an occupational pension scheme. The condition applies only to processing of sensitive data relating to the health of a parent, grandparent, great-grandparent or sibling of an insured person or member of a pension scheme. A further qualification is that the processing must be necessary in a case where the organisation cannot reasonably be expected to obtain the explicit consent of the parent, grandparent, great-grandparent or sibling and is not aware that they have withheld their consent.

In addition, the personal information relating to the parent, grandparent, great-grandparent or sibling must not be used to support measures or decisions in connection with the parent, grandparent, great grandparent or sibling. So, information relating to the medical history of near relatives may be processed for the purposes of assessing the risk posed by a person making an insurance proposal or being considered for entry into pension scheme membership or benefits. The information cannot be processed to make a decision relating to the parent, grandparent, great-grandparent or sibling themselves.

SENSITIVE DATA IN INSURANCE CLAIMS

At the most basic level an insurance policy is a promise to pay a claim if an insured event occurs during the period of insurance and none of the policy exclusions apply. There are implications when processing personal information in relation to an insurance claim as, inevitably, the claim notification and management processes will elicit personal information additional to that already held, including sensitive data and data relating to third parties.

When processing sensitive categories of claims data, the most appropriate condition is that the parties involved give explicit consent to the processing. This is complicated by the circumstances of claims reporting; third parties will almost certainly not have had sight of subject information provided previously; for example, an employee who claims on the employers' liability insurance will probably not have seen the subject information provided to the employer when personal information was supplied in connection with underwriting the policy. Similarly, an individual involved in a motor accident may make a third-party claim on a motor insurance policy to which they are not a party. This means that the claimant's decision to notify the details of the claim, including sensitive data, is not fully informed.

To a degree, the organisation may rely on a common sense approach, that the individuals concerned are aware of the purposes for which their personal information will be processed because it is submitted in connection with a claim on an insurance policy and that explicit consent to the processing of sensitive data may be inferred from their actions.

The matter is further complicated where a third party acts on behalf of the claimant, for example, a solicitor or a family member. In such cases, the personal data is obtained indirectly and slightly different rules apply in that the third party (solicitor or family member) is responsible for obtaining the explicit consent of the person to whom the personal data relates.

In claims management, another applicable condition for fair processing of sensitive data is that the processing is necessary to exercise or defend a legal right. The claimant is exercising a legal right when bringing a claim under a liability insurance policy, for example, occupier's liability, employer's liability and motor insurance. The insurer and its agents are assisting the insured party to defend its legal rights.

SENSITIVE DATA IN OTHER AREAS

The following are other areas that involve the processing of sensitive data:

- health details of applicants for, and customers with, loans, mortgages, insurance;

- health details of close family of applicants for life insurance;

- health details of insurance claimants;

- health details of visitors who have an accident on insured premises;

- race of employees/staff for equal opportunities monitoring;

- health details of employees/staff for statutory and company sick pay schemes, and to meet health and safety requirements;

- trade union membership of employees.

Each activity must be justified by reference to one or more of the conditions for processing sensitive data. So, for example:

- Health details of applicants for loans, mortgages, insurance are processed with their explicit consent.

- Health details of customers with loans, mortgages or insurance are processed with explicit consent. If they experience hardship due to ill health, they will report their problems to the organisation and consent to the processing of that information in connection with the administration of their account.

- Health details of close family of applicants for life insurance are processed in reliance on the insurance and pensions conditions set out in the Sensitive Data Order.

- Health details of insurance claimants are processed in reliance on the condition justifying processing in connection with defending legal rights.

- Health details of visitors who have an accident on the premises are likewise justified by reference to the defence of legal rights or with explicit consent.

- Race of employees/staff for equal opportunities monitoring is justified by reference to the Equal Opportunities condition.

- Health details of employees/staff for statutory and company sick pay schemes, and to meet health and safety requirements are processed by reference to the legal obligation on the organisation as an employer.

- Trade union membership of employees are processed with the explicit consent of the employees.

Although there is no provision for organisations to state publicly which of the conditions for fair processing of sensitive data they rely upon, it is still recommended that organisations consider them and document any initial thoughts on the applicability of the conditions to their processing activities. These will be invaluable if the organisation is involved in a dispute over fair processing and is asked to explain its fair processing position to the Information Commissioner.

CONCLUSION

Organisations that process sensitive categories of information are required to authorise their processing activity by reference to one or more conditions for the fair processing of sensitive data set out in one of the schedules to the Act. The conditions allow processing only in very restricted and prescribed circumstances, but the current list, supplemented by the Sensitive Data Order, appears to cover the processing activity relating to sensitive categories of data undertaken routinely by financial services organisations.

CHAPTER 16

Record-keeping and the Fourth and Fifth Principles

The standards for information management are laid down in the data protection principles. Several of the data protection principles impact on record-keeping; in particular, the third principle requires personal data to be adequate, relevant and not excessive and the fourth principle requires that it be accurate and kept up to date where necessary. The fifth principle imposes an obligation to retain personal data for no longer than is necessary for the purpose for which it is processed. The issue of security, having wider implications than document and information security, is covered in the next chapter.

ENSURING ACCURACY

The requirement that personal data be accurate is not absolute. Where personal data is inaccurate, but the data controller can show that the information in the data is reproduced in its records exactly as it was obtained, then there is no breach of data protection law. So, for example, if an insurance proposal is completed using inaccurate information that the broker or insurance company believes to be true, then neither the broker nor the insurance company is in breach of data protection principles even though their records include inaccurate information. Similarly, if information is inaccurately recorded in the broker's office and passed on to the insurance company, the latter is not in breach, although its records are inaccurate. However, there is a duty to take reasonable steps to ensure the accuracy of personal data.

Where possible, organisations should use automated means to verify personal data; for example, computer systems should be programmed so that the current year is not accepted in a date of birth data entry field. Postcode and telephone number data entry fields can be automatically restricted to a limited number of digits to assist in maintaining accuracy when recording personal data. Databases are available from the Royal Mail (see Chapter 14) that automatically provide address details when prompted by entering the postcode. All of these automated systems can help to reduce data entry errors.

There is also a general duty on organisations to ensure that data collection and entry operators are trained and supervised by staff who can use common sense when dealing with personal data and, if it appears that information may be inaccurate, to investigate further rather than accepting the information at face value.

Where an organisation holds information that is known or believed to be inaccurate, it may want to retain the information in its original form for its own purposes. The information might indicate an attempted fraud or show a discrepancy that has not been satisfactorily explained. In such circumstances, the organisation is not compelled to amend the information but it should record the discrepancy and the date it was noted.

If the Information Commissioner investigates an allegation that personal data held by an organisation is inaccurate, the issues that would be considered include:[1]

- The significance of the inaccuracy. Has it caused or is it likely to cause damage or distress to the individual?

- The source from which the inaccurate information was obtained. Was it reasonable for the organisation to rely on information received from that source?

- Any steps taken to verify the information and whether the organisation attempted to check its accuracy with another source. Would it have been reasonable to ask the individual (where information is obtained from a third party), either at the time of collection or at another convenient opportunity, whether the information was accurate?

- The procedures for data entry and for ensuring that the system itself does not introduce inaccuracies into the data.

- The procedures followed by the organisation when the inaccuracy came to light. Were the data corrected as soon as the inaccuracy became apparent? Was the correction passed on to any third parties to whom the inaccurate data may already have been disclosed? Did the inaccuracy have any other consequences in the period before it was corrected? If so, what has the organisation done about those consequences?

KEEPING PERSONAL INFORMATION UP TO DATE

Personal information must be kept up to date, but only where it is necessary to do so. A record intended to provide a snapshot of circumstances as at a given date will not

---

1   Information Commissioner (1994) *The Guidelines: Third Series*, part 4. London: Data Protection Registrar. This was in relation to the Data Protection Act 1984, but still relevant to the fourth principle (in November 1994 this was the fifth principle).

need to be updated. For example, most organisations require customers and clients to keep them advised of changes in their circumstances, such as change of address and change of name. The client record should show the correct current address; other documentation or records might show previous addresses and this is acceptable.

There are circumstances where it is essential that information is up to date. Current contact details are essential information; without a current address the organisation is unable to correspond with the client, probably in breach of its terms and conditions and FSA regulations relating to the provision of account information.

Up-to-date information is critical when it is processed to determine whether or not an applicant is credit-worthy. This applies to both the lender, and to any other organisation involved in supplying information, such as a credit reference agency. This is an area where a consumer could suffer damage (by not being offered credit) if personal data is inaccurate. The sort of factors the Information Commissioner would take into consideration when assessing a complaint that a consumer had been disadvantaged would include:[2]

- any record of when the personal information was obtained and updated;

- whether the organisation was aware or should have been aware that the personal information may not be up to date;

- any procedures to update personal information and their effectiveness;

- whether or not the non-currency of the personal information is likely to cause damage or distress to the individual concerned.

OTHER GUIDANCE

The following best practice guidelines are taken from the Direct Marketing Association guidelines for data management.[3] The guidelines are directed at DMA members, but they indicate the practices that help to establish a compliant personal information file.

- When carrying out a direct mailshot, a change of address file should be used to validate addresses before they are mailed.

- Third-party marketers should ensure that their clients register as a data controller and comply with the requirements of the seventh data protection

2   *Legal Guidance*, para. 3.4.
3   *Best Practice Guidelines – Data in Direct Marketing*, section F, 'Name and address conversion and cleaning', section B, 'Data protection and legislation', section C, 'Caring for personal data'.

principle when using marketers in the role of data processors. Section B of the guidelines includes suggested contract terms.

- The fourth data protection principle underlines the management of personal information. The database owner should be conscious of the time sensitivity of information and the fact that it may become less relevant over time. The DMA recommends a cycle of updating and refreshing customer information before sending a communication.

- Address management procedures should be in place to maintain accurate customer addresses. These should include updating postal addresses using software that references the Royal Mail's Postcode Address File; using customer notifications of change of address or employing proprietary change of address and suppression files.

KEEPING PERSONAL INFORMATION FOR NO LONGER THAN IS NECESSARY

Data protection law does not set down minimum or maximum periods for which personal information should be retained. The legal requirement is simply to keep personal information for no longer than is necessary for the purpose or purposes for which it is processed; how long depends on the purposes for which it is processed. The 1980 Limitation Act sets a 6-year period from the termination of a contract as the maximum period during which a claim under the contract can be made. Therefore contractual documents and records relating to the performance of a contract are generally kept for 6 years from the date on which the contract terminated. Equally valid are the much longer retention periods applying to certain records required for health and safety purposes.

Below is a table with some suggested document retention periods together with an indication of the legal reasons behind the suggested time period. The table gives an indication of the diversity of laws applicable to document retention, and is not designed to be adopted wholesale as an information retention policy.

These are retention periods largely set down by law but other areas may not have such clear authority for retaining records. The basic principle is that the organisation needs to retain documents and information for as long as is necessary for it to meet its own lawful objectives. Note that the requirement relates to 'necessity' rather than 'choice'; the organisation must be able to demonstrate a real need for records, rather than a preference or a requirement based on incompetence or unwillingness to delete or purge records.

Record	Retention period	Reason for retention
Company law books, board and member minutes, registers, circulars to shareholders, stock and share transfer forms	Permanently	Company law
Proxy forms and polling cards	1 month from date of meeting unless a poll is demanded, then 1 year from the data of the meeting	Company law
Dividend and interest mandates	Until the account is closed	
Contracts with clients, suppliers, agents, franchise agreements, licensing agreements, rental and loan agreements, indemnities and guarantees	6 years from the date of termination of the contract or liability	Statute of Limitations
Patent and trade mark records	Permanently	
Accounting records	6 years from date of reports and records	Company law, Inland Revenue and VAT requirements
Personnel records	Summary information 10 years after employment ceases	To respond to reference requests or enquiries from DSS, Inland Revenue and so on
Salary details and tax returns	6 years from relevant date	Inland Revenue requirements
Accident books	Permanently	

Table continued overleaf

Record	Retention period	Reason for retention
Pension trust deeds and rules, trustees' minutes, investment records, actuarial valuations and contributions records	Permanently	Pensions law
Insurance policies and certificates	Permanently	
Claims correspondence	3 years after settlement of the claim	Statute of Limitations

CONCLUSION

Several initiatives are useful to help to keep records compliant with the data protection principles. Procedures and staff trained to understand the issues can assist with document retention and purging of records to keep them up to date and relevant. System-based solutions would include restricted data entry fields to help reduce inaccuracies and data cleansing exercises to match up postcodes or to suppress unwanted mailings or returns.

Document retention remains a major issue for many organisations. Where possible, organisations should ensure that retention periods are commensurate with those adopted by others in the industry. If there are specific business reasons to support longer or shorter retention periods than those that are standard in the industry, document the reasons why. All document retention periods should be justifiable and the justification evidenced in writing for future reference. When considering document retention, include computer files as well as paper files. Ensure that computer systems allow personal data to be deleted permanently. Some systems have the facility for automatic purging guidelines to be built into the record-keeping system; this is helpful so long as there is provision for a manual override when required.

CHAPTER 17

Security: The Practical Implications of the Seventh Principle

Maintaining security is a key concern for any organisation involved in financial services, both for itself and for its customers. Banks and building societies, insurance companies and investment houses have been targeted for fraud and theft, with threats coming from both outside and within organisations. The primary concern of financial institutions is to maintain the integrity of financial systems rather than the integrity of personal information; nevertheless there is a significant overlap between the two objectives.

The common law duty of confidentiality is closest to the statutory duty of care owed in relation to personal information. It is generally accepted that the duty of confidentiality is owed to clients and customers across the financial services industry. Paragraph 11 of *The Banking Code* outlines the duty of confidentiality that financial institutions owe to their customers.[1] *The Banking Code* enjoins its subscribers to treat all personal information as private and confidential, not revealing customers' names and addresses or details about their accounts, other than in the exceptional cases allowed by law. *The Banking Code* reflects the overriding duty of confidentiality that banks and building societies owe to their customers. The provisions of *The Banking Code* are mirrored in codes of practice issued by the ABI and professional standards established by other industry bodies.

Add to the duty of confidentiality the prospect of criminal sanctions for unlawfully disclosing personal information under the Data Protection Act 1998 (the Act) and you have a complete picture of security issues in relation to personal information.

UNAUTHORISED AND UNLAWFUL PROCESSING

The Act requires organisations to take appropriate organisational and technical measures to protect personal information against unauthorised or unlawful processing. The term 'unauthorised' could be applied to two sets of circumstances.

---

1   *Tournier* v. *National Provincial and Union Bank of England* [1924] 1KB461.

First, where processing is outside of the authority of the organisation. The organisation's authority depends on subject information provided to individuals whose personal information is processed and its data protection registration entries. Second, where processing is undertaken by employees and agents of the organisation who are acting outside of the organisation's delegated authority.

Where personal information is processed by the organisation outside its authority, the processing is likely to constitute a breach of the Data Protection Principles.[2] Where an agent or employee processes personal information without proper authority from the organisation, the activity is likely to constitute a criminal offence as well as a breach of the data protection principles. Unauthorised processing by an employee is likely to constitute a breach of security, especially where an organisation establishes compliance procedures but these are either not followed or not implemented correctly by its employees.

In a recent incident involving HFC Bank[3] an email was sent to a number of its loan customers that mistakenly included the email addresses of all other recipients. This constituted a disclosure of personal information that should have been kept confidential; although the processing of personal information was authorised by the bank the way in which it was carried out was unauthorised. The breach of procedures that resulted in the unauthorised processing amounts to a breach of security; neither the procedures nor the supervision of employees was sufficient to prevent the unauthorised disclosure. In this case, the disclosure of personal information was also a breach of the obligation of confidentiality owed to clients, so the processing was both unlawful and unauthorised.

This incident also demonstrates that the objective of securing the integrity of financial systems is not quite the same as securing the integrity of personal information. There was no financial loss to customers in the HFC Bank case but a breach of confidentiality. Data protection law is all about confidentiality, privacy and fair processing.

A similar case of unauthorised processing of personal data by an employee involved a complaint against a debt collection company.[4] In the process of collecting the debt, an employee of the company disclosed information about the individual's account to members of his family. This included details of how much was owed. The Information Commissioner found on assessment that it was likely that the disclosure had

---

2 The second principle requires that personal data be processed in accordance with specified purposes and not in any manner inconsistent with those purposes.

3 Reported in BBC news online on 25 September 2004. Available from news.bbc.co.uk/1/hi/programmes/moneybox/3689480.stm.

4 Details taken from Information Commissioner's 2003 *Annual Report and Accounts*.

contravened the seventh data protection principle. Although the company ensured that its staff underwent induction training on data protection issues, there had been a breach of procedures and training in making the disclosure. This amounted to a breach of security and hence the seventh principle.

SECURITY MEASURES

The elements of an appropriate security policy would include the technical and organisational measures as outlined in Chapter 10 on the seventh principle.

Some activities present a specific risk or set of risks and specific measures should be adopted to deal with these. For example:

- Home working policies including security aspects and the supply of computer equipment for home workers to ensure that adequate firewall and virus protection is in place as well as the required functionality of the server.

- Laptop, hand-held computer and mobile phone security policies to protect personal information stored in such devices. Use of encryption and password protection where available. The latest developments in the mobile phone industry include high memory capacity smartphones. A recent survey of taxi drivers showed that thousands of valuable mobile phones, personal digital assistants (PDAs) and laptops are left in taxis every day.

- Additional log-on requirements for shared computers and strict clean desk policies for shared desks where staff 'hot desk' or share jobs.

- Strict procedures and regular monitoring to ensure that documents are not left on shared printers, perhaps even designating a responsible member of staff to police the printer and remove and deliver its output.

- Secure intranet links between offices or branches that need to exchange personal information electronically.

- Secure Internet links for customers who perform tasks or submit personal information online.

- Warranties and contractual obligations for courier firms used to transfer personal information between locations. Employing only reputable courier firms.

- Warranties and contractual obligations for private investigator firms used to trace debtors or establish the veracity of insurance claims. Employing only reputable firms and monitoring their activities.

CRIMINAL OFFENCES

One additional element that data protection law brings to security issues generally is that unauthorised obtaining or disclosure of personal information is a criminal offence,[5] whereas breach of confidentiality is a civil matter. Individuals as well as organisations may be held liable under data protection law for criminal offences. This fact can be used to reinforce messages about client confidentiality given to staff. There is no requirement for unauthorised obtaining or disclosure of information to be malicious; in a case involving a Special Constable working for Dorset Police a fine of £1000 was levied against the individual for using a police database for unauthorised access to investigate people she knew.

PHISHING

At the time of writing, the latest security challenge to the financial services industry is 'phishing'. This involves fraudsters setting up Internet websites and sending bogus emails to consumers that purport to emanate from legitimate institutions, principally banks and building societies. The aim of the emails is to deceive consumers into revealing their account details, including security passwords. The fraudsters may plunder the bank or building society accounts of deceived consumers or even steal their identity, obtaining credit cards and loans in the false identity. According to the Home Office, identity theft is now the fastest growing crime and costs the UK in excess of £1.3 billion a year.

In October 2004 the Anti-Phishing Working Group reported 6597 new phishing email messages, representing a monthly growth rate of 36 per cent. The messages targeted 46 different brands. Of the institutions targeted, 73 per cent are banks and financial institutions.

Financial institutions currently indemnify consumers against loss due to computer fraud, subject to the consumer adhering to some basic safety precautions. By offering Internet services such as online banking, financial services institutions must stand the risk of losses due to fraud.

The seventh principle requires security measures to be 'state of the art', but, unfortunately, 'state of the art' currently cannot fully obstruct phishing activities. To comply with the seventh principle, institutions that offer online services must ensure that they keep pace with technological and organisational security developments, perhaps most importantly with those developments embraced by others in the sector, so as not to fall behind in comparative terms. The Information Commissioner would

---

5   The Data Protection Act 1998, section 55.

certainly consider benchmarking 'state of the art' on what other, similar, organisations are doing.

CHIP AND PIN

Also at the time of writing, debit and credit card issuers are implementing the migration to 'chip and pin' technology. In place of a signature to confirm a purchase by card in a retail store or garage, consumers are now able to enter their security number to authorise the transaction. The rationale is that a signature may be forged, if a fraudster took possession of a bank card with a signature on the reverse or obtained the carbon from a Visa or Mastercard authorisation slip. A security password, made up of numbers selected by the consumer should be more secure so long as the consumer selects numbers at random (a birth date might be too easy to guess if the fraudster knows their victim) and never discloses or writes down their chosen number.

Probably the key aspect of introducing 'chip and pin' is that the responsibility for helping to prevent fraudulent activity shifts towards the consumer. *The Banking Code* provides that banks and building societies will act immediately to prevent cards being used if the consumer notifies them that a cheque book, passbook, card or electronic purse has been lost or stolen, or that someone else knows relevant PIN or other security information.[6] It also requires customers to keep financial institutions up to date with changes of circumstances, to check account statements, to take care not to keep cheque book and cards together, to keep card, PIN, and passwords confidential, to choose PIN carefully and not to write them down, and to keep cards safe.[7] In respect of liability, a consumer will not be held liable for the full extent of losses due to lost or stolen cards and so on unless the consumer has either acted fraudulently or without reasonable care.[8]

In practice, the first hurdle that a victim will face is to convince the financial institution that they have not disclosed the security password or written it down. The circumstances will not favour the consumer as it is highly unlikely that a fraudster would be able to select numbers at random to match a security password coincidentally. Already consumer groups are expressing concerns in relation to this issue. It shows that the requirement for security can include the individual as well as the organisations that process personal information. Quite how far this will develop remains to be seen.

---

6   *The Banking Code*, para. 9.15.
7   *The Banking Code*, para. 12.
8   *The Banking Code*, para. 12.10.

THE SECURITY REQUIREMENTS OF BEING AN OUTSOURCE SERVICE PROVIDER

Increasingly organisations are prepared to outsource specific functions where the cost of undertaking those functions within the organisation is higher than the cost of employing an outsource service provider to perform the function on its behalf. For many organisations this presents a business opportunity. In those cases where the service provided involves processing personal information, there may be compliance implications under the seventh principle. There is now a statutory duty on organisations that employ service providers to check the organisational and technical security measures in place to ensure the security of personal information processed on their behalf. There is also a requirement for written contracts with subcontractors and outsource service suppliers incorporating two specific data protection terms. The implications for data controllers using outsource providers is discussed in Chapter 19.

As data protection law does not recognise trading groups of companies, sister and associated companies in a group are treated as independent third parties. Technically, a group structure may involve one or more of the companies in the group acting as an outsource service provider to other companies in the group. This will bring the seventh principle into effect as between group companies.

The sections that follow consider the type of outsourcing relationship that give rise to the compliance issue under the seventh principle and suggest steps that service providers can take to assist their clients in meeting the compliance requirements.

Not all outsourcing arrangements involve processing personal information. Equally the new statutory duty does not apply to all outsourcing relationships, it only applies where one party processes on behalf of the other, acting on its instructions without autonomy to make decisions in relation to the personal information. Deciding whether or not an organisation is a data processor is a matter of fact in each case. There is more information about how to recognise relevant data controller to data processor relationships in Chapter 10 on the seventh principle.

THE IMPLICATIONS OF BEING A DATA PROCESSOR

The Act and the data protection principles do not prima facie regulate the activities of data processors. The seventh principle applies so that organisations are held responsible for the compliance of their data processors. Appropriate security measures are the key part of that obligation. Security compliance measures must be policed by the organisation.

In addition, there is a statutory requirement for written contracts between an organisation and its data processors. Specifically, an organisation is not to be regarded as complying with the seventh principle unless there is a contract in writing that specifies that the data processor will only act on instructions from the organisation and that requires the data processor to comply with obligations equivalent to those imposed on a data controller by the seventh principle.[9]

These issues are considered in detail in Chapter 10.

Elements of a positive position on data protection

Identifying data processors is not always clear cut and it is preferable for the parties to reach agreement as to their respective roles and obligations at the start of the relationship. Outsource service providers should discuss the position with legal advisers and the Information Commissioner's Office to obtain a clear view and put that view forward to clients and prospects. They should also consider adopting and publicising a statement of policy on data protection, ensuring that it has the support of senior management. This policy should be implemented by:

- introducing and monitoring procedures for staff who handle personal information as part of their job;

- ensuring that appropriate training is given to staff with a practical bias so that they understand data protection implications for their job and the ramifications of breaches, including the potential for personal liability;

- paying particular attention to temporary workers, contract staff and new starters and make sure that the company's policy and procedures relating to data protection are effectively communicated to these categories of employee;

- supervising and monitoring staff to ensure that procedures are adequate, practical and being followed in practice;

- ensuring that appropriate security measures are in place;

- carrying out independent audits from time to time and making the resulting reports available to existing clients and new prospects.

CONCLUSION

Financial institutions need to have security measures in place to maintain the integrity of their financial systems. In addition, the duty of client and customer confidentiality extends the security requirement to include records of personal information. There is little that data protection compliance can require of financial institutions that is not

---

9   The Data Protection Act 1998, Part II, Schedule 1, para. 12.

already required to meet other obligations. Only in relation to the criminal offences under the Act is any additional knowledge required and additional activity in terms of alerting employees to the existence of the criminal offences of unlawful obtaining and disclosing of personal information and ensuring that they are aware that personal liability for individuals is a feature of the Act.

The latest security scare relates to phishing, but while financial institutions are under a duty to seek out the best means to combat fraudulent activity, the data protection requirement to provide security for personal information is not absolute. The requirement is for appropriate organisational and technical measures, what is 'appropriate' being determined by the circumstances. The only danger is if an organisation were to fail to keep abreast of technological development in its industry. What is appropriate will partly be determined by what the competition considers is appropriate. Liaison with other organisations in the industry and joint fraud prevention initiatives are therefore recommended courses of action.

The seventh data protection principle imposes a requirement for data controllers to ensure an appropriate level of security for personal data in its control. This includes personal data held and processed by service providers on behalf of the data controller. In the last analysis, the security requirements imposed by the seventh principle are fundamental business requirements for organisations in the financial services industry. Security is more about meeting business needs than meeting regulatory requirements. As ever, the regulatory requirements impose a need for documenting compliance measures and there are specific requirements where processing of personal data is outsourced to data processors. This chapter has considered the implications for service providers competing for business that will be subject to the seventh principle and suggests some ways in which a proactive organisation could benefit from a positive position in relation to data protection.

CHAPTER 18

The Exercise of Subject Rights and the Sixth Principle

The Data Protection Act 1998 (the Act) gives individuals a number of rights in relation to personal information relating to them. The best known is the right of access to personal information. This right was established under the 1984 Act and most people are familiar with it. Other rights have been created under the 1998 Act. The one that is exercised with increasing frequency is the right to prevent processing for purposes of direct marketing. One of the responsibilities of the Information Commissioner is to increase public awareness of data protection rights and there have been initiatives to introduce the subject in schools, so the exercise of subject rights is an area that is likely to increase in importance.

As with other contact during the relationship with the client, the exercise of subject rights is an opportunity to communicate with clients and to impress them with quality service. The key to providing a quality service when dealing with the exercise of subject rights is to be able to identify when they are being exercised and proceed accordingly. All staff who have customer contact must be able to recognise the exercise of subject rights under the Act even though the consumer may not be aware that they are exercising a statutory right. Training is the only way to alert staff to the existence of data protection subject rights and to ensure that the exercise of rights is recognised and facilitated.

Subject rights may also be exercised by employees in relation to their employer. The Employment Code recommends that employers tell their employees about their rights under the Act, including the right of access to information on their personnel or HR file.

The sixth data protection principle enshrines subject rights and the organisation's duty to process personal data in accordance with those rights. The technical aspects of subject rights are considered in depth in Chapter 9 on the sixth data protection principle. However, a summary of the key points of each is set out below together with guidance on handling enquiries.

SUBJECT ACCESS REQUEST

As noted in Chapter 9 on the sixth data protection principle, individuals have a right to a copy of any information comprising 'personal data' relating to them that is in the control of the organisation. The right of access relates to the information comprising personal information, not a copy of every document that features it. So although it may generally be quicker and easier to copy an entire file relating to an individual on request, it may be that the only personal information contained in a file of correspondence is the individual's name and address. In these circumstances, it is permissible to simply provide the name and address as information that is personal information in the possession of the organisation.

The ruling in the *Durant* v. *Financial Services Authority* case[1] significantly reduced the potential information that might constitute 'personal data'. Following Durant, information that can be excluded from a subject access request now includes passing references to the individual and documents or files that are not directly concerned with that individual. Given this narrower definition, organisations may find it more beneficial to review files of documents to extract relevant information rather than simply copying or printing the entire file.

Overall, the exceptions to subject access, that is those cases where the organisation may withhold information from the individual making the request, apply in relation to individual pieces of information rather than exempting the organisation from compliance with the entire request.

The most commonly applicable exemption applies to personal information relating to another individual (a 'third party'), where that individual has not consented to the disclosure of the information to the person making the request and it is not reasonable to disclose the information without their consent. This situation arises in particular in relation to employment references. A referee may have been approached for a reference 'in confidence' but the organisation that sought the reference is the party that will decide whether or not to reveal the information in the reference if requested by the subject of it.

In practice, this can put the data controller in an unenviable position. A subject access request has been made and relevant information also identifies and relates to a third party. If the third party withholds consent to the disclosure of their personal data in order to comply with the request, the data controller must make a decision to withhold or disclose the personal data. In either event, one of the parties will be unhappy with the action taken. This is particularly so in relation to personal

---

1   See Chapter 3 for the facts of the case.

references. A reference may be provided under a promise of confidentiality, but its content may be such that the organisation has no choice but to reveal it to the data subject, as the effect of the reference on that individual is significant and harmful. Given the importance of references for 'approved persons' and the overriding considerations of 'full and frank disclosure' to prospective employers, the likely impact of an adverse reference will be significant to the individual concerned and it is hard to envisage how their rights could be less significant than those of the referee in these circumstances.

Information that should be included in any response to a subject access request includes:

- Opinions as well as matters of fact. Under the 1984 Act opinions could be excluded but the 1998 Act specifically includes them.

- Statements of the organisation's intentions regarding the individual making the subject access request, except in relation to negotiations between the organisation and the individual.

- Information held in structured paper files that is easily located and retrieved.

- Information held in a variety of media including on audio and video tape, microfiche, imaged documents as well as computer files.

- Information held in backup data.

In general, the organisation should aim to comply with a request for access made under the Act. Although there are exemptions from the information required to be provided, these should be used sparingly with the emphasis on disclosure wherever possible. Only if an individual is unable to verify their identity to the reasonable satisfaction of the organisation, or if they make repeated request for access, may it decline to provide any information in response to an access enquiry.

THE MECHANICS OF DEALING WITH A SUBJECT ACCESS REQUEST

When responding to a subject access request the organisation must:

- provide confirmation that the organisation holds personal data relating to the enquirer;

- advise the enquirer of the purposes for which their personal data is processed;

- advise the enquirer of the sources of the personal data.

In addition, on request the enquirer is entitled to be advised:

- if the data is subject to any automated decision-making process;

- of the logic involved in any automated processing in certain circumstances.

A charge of up to £10 may be made towards administration costs and the organisation does not have to comply with the request until any such charge is paid. The organisation may reasonably require proof of identity from the enquirer in order to verify their identity and to assist in locating the information sought. A pre-designed form is often used to ensure that the enquirer receives a speedy response and that the right questions are asked about their relationship with the organisation and the nature of the enquiry. It can be useful to check recent complaint files as many subject access requests arise when an individual has a dispute with the organisation. This background may help to identify what information is sought by the individual in particular.

When responding to a subject access request, an explanation of codes and references used in the information must be provided if their meaning is not clear. The information must be provided in legible, permanent form unless an alternative is agreed with the data subject or if providing it in permanent form would involve disproportionate effort. The term 'disproportionate effort' is not defined but is a matter of judgement in each case. Guidance from the Information Commissioner suggests that factors such as the cost of providing a permanent copy of the information, the length of time likely to be taken to produce it and how difficult it may be for the organisation to provide it should be balanced against the rights of the individual in each case.[2]

The organisation may adopt a separate procedure for employee subject access requests. Employees will regularly require different pieces of information from the HR department; for example, to check on the amount of holiday entitlement left, or when seeking confirmation of details from contracts of employment, and so on. In addition, employees are usually party to much of the information that is held on the HR file, for example appraisal information is usually shared with the employee and the content of any disciplinary notices will have been disclosed in writing. Therefore a request from an employee for access to information held on their personnel file may not need to be treated as a subject access request.

An employer is able to negotiate with the employee about the information required and the form that it should take; for example, an employee might be given their

---

2   *Legal Guidance*, para. 4.1.

personnel file to browse through in a confidential environment and allowed to take copies of information on request. This might be preferable to providing a photocopy of the entire file and agreeable to both parties. However, the employee has the right to insist that the subject access procedure is followed.

PROBLEMS WITH SUBJECT ACCESS

The key problem reported to the Information Commissioner by individuals is that organisations fail to respond to a subject access request within the specified period. Organisations are allowed 40 days from receipt of the request to respond with full disclosure. This is one reason why the ability to identify when a subject access request is being made is so critical. The organisation has a limited period in which to verify the identity of the person making the subject access request and to locate all relevant information.

THE RIGHT TO PREVENT PROCESSING FOR THE PURPOSES OF DIRECT MARKETING

Individuals have the right to prevent processing of personal information relating to them for the purposes of direct marketing.[3] An individual may make a written request at any time to require an organisation to cease, or not to begin, processing their personal information for the purposes of direct marketing.

The organisation has a 'reasonable' period of time in which to amend records and prospect databases to comply with the request. Generally, 28 days is the period allowed for processing registrations with the Mailing Preference Service. After 28 days, the individual is entitled to assume that direct marketers have amended their records. It is a reasonable time period to adopt for dealing with the exercise of the same right under the Act.

POSSIBLE PROBLEM AREAS

The risk is that an objection to marketing activity may not be actioned effectively. This may be because the marketing database does not have the functionality to prevent mailings or because there are several marketing databases in use at any one time. A way must be found to ensure that marketing objections are respected and that marketing to that individual ceases. If a computer system will not distinguish between persons on the database who have objected to marketing and those who have not, then delete the marketing address on the file or keep a separate list of objections to match against future mailings. If there are several different marketing databases, document a procedure to notify the database 'owners' of the receipt of an objection

---

3   The Data Protection Act 1998, section 11.

and require confirmation from each that the objection has been actioned. The right to object to the use of personal information for direct marketing is an absolute right, the organisation is obliged to respect a request to cease direct marketing and there are no defences for failing to respect it. Organisations must find a way to action such requests.

Another issue when dealing with requests to cease the use of personal information for purposes of direct marketing is whether a request received by one trading company in a group applies also to other trading companies in that group. Many financial services organisations are groups of companies for legal and regulatory reasons as well as functional reasons. Separate corporate entities might maintain separate marketing lists and will certainly have separate client lists and it is common for cross-marketing to take place, where one trading company promotes the products or services of another in the same group. How far an objection to direct marketing should be implemented in other group company marketing databases depends on the expectations of the individual who raises the objection. If companies in the group present themselves as a marketing group with a common brand and house style, then it is likely that the individual will expect a marketing objection to apply to prevent all further direct marketing by any of the trading companies in the group unless specified otherwise.

THE RIGHT TO OBJECT TO DECISIONS TAKEN BY AUTOMATED MEANS

Under Section 12 of the Act, an individual is entitled to object to decisions taken by automated means in circumstances where the decision significantly affects that individual.

The organisation is required to disclose that decisions are being made by automated means and the logic of the decision-making process if requested by the individual. However, an organisation does not have to comply if the disclosure of the logic involved in the automated processing would constitute the disclosure of a 'trade secret'.

Examples of business areas likely to be affected are credit scoring and underwriting systems. So there may be legitimate concerns that disclosure of the logic behind an automated decision-making process might enable a fraudster to select against the organisation in an area where automated decision-making processes apply. The organisation's objective is to prevent the disclosure of information that could assist an enquirer in perpetrating a fraud by manipulating responses to credit scoring or underwriting questions to select against the organisation. Consider, though, that just because non-disclosure is in the best interests of the organisation it does not necessarily follow that it is a trade secret.

In relation to HR, employees may object to automated psychometric tests and automated scoring or marking of tests and exams. Applicants for jobs may object to automated recruitment processes online.

The risk is that a member of staff receiving a complaint about a decision taken by automated means may not realise that the Act is relevant to the issue. Training is the key to raising staff awareness so that the exercise of this right can be identified and dealt with correctly.

There is also a risk that disclosing the logic behind a decision taken by automated means will reveal too much information about the organisation's credit scoring or underwriting policies. This information may be used by fraudsters to select against the organisation or by competitors to cherry pick the better risks. A suggested solution is to describe in fairly general terms the areas where automated decisions are taken with an indication of the type of factors the system takes into account when making the decision. A blunt refusal to supply any information is likely only to lead to frustration on the part of the enquirer who may then take the matter further.

THE RIGHT TO PREVENT PROCESSING LIKELY TO CAUSE DAMAGE OR DISTRESS

An individual may also prevent processing likely to cause damage or distress to themselves or another person.[4] The notice must be in writing, setting out the reasons why processing is causing or is likely to cause substantial damage or distress to themselves or another and further, that the damage or distress is unwarranted. A period of 21 days is allowed for the organisation to respond. Its response should set out any reasons it has for not complying with the request to cease processing, bearing in mind that the final arbiter may be the courts.

There are exceptions to the right to object to processing likely to cause damage or distress; for example, if the individual has consented to the processing or if the processing is necessary for the performance of a contract to which the individual is a party or to meet an obligation to which the organisation is subject, other than a contractual obligation.

The risk here is that staff may not make the link between a complaint by an individual and the fact that they have a right to object to certain processing activity under the data protection act that involves certain procedural requirements. The definition of 'processing' is so wide as to encompass any activity involving personal data so that any complaint about mismanagement or misstatement may involve the

---

4   The Data Protection Act 1998, section 10.

exercise of the right to object to processing likely to cause damage or distress. It is suggested that if an individual takes the time and trouble to write and complain, they are likely to have suffered damage or distress.

Most organisations will reply to a complaint setting out their side of the dispute, which should include the reasons why it acts in the way complained of. This should meet the statutory requirement in relation to the right to object to certain personal data processing. A further suggestion is that the internal complaints handling procedure should include a reference to this subject right to remind staff who deal with complaints to think about possible data protection ramifications in every complaint they handle.

THE RIGHT TO COMPENSATION

Any individual who suffers harm by reason of contravention of any of the requirements of the Act is entitled to compensation from the data controller. This right is exercised via the Courts. The process is likely to start with a complaint which, if not handled correctly, will escalate into a request for compensation. Many solicitors are now aware of the value of subject access when dealing with a compensation claim; they find it useful to have sight of the other side's papers to look for grounds on which to bring or bolster a case. Alternatively, the individual might approach the Information Commissioner with a request for assessment. This means an investigation of the circumstances surrounding the complaint by the Information Commissioner. The outcome is an official view as to whether or not the organisation was likely to have been in breach of data protection law in the circumstances described. This is valuable evidence when the individual applies to the Court for compensation.

The risks here all relate to how complaints and the exercise of other subject rights are handled. If the organisation has a robust procedure for dealing effectively with complaints and has invested in training for staff to help them to recognise the exercise of data protection rights, then it significantly reduces the risk that it will be pursued for compensation for breaches of data protection law.

As with any request for compensation, negotiation towards an early settlement of disputes can reduce the eventual exposure. A suggested strategy is to ensure that staff involved in a dispute are not also made responsible for handling the complaint. An objective viewpoint is more likely to yield a negotiated settlement.

RIGHTS IN RELATION TO INACCURATE DATA

Individuals have rights to require the rectification, blocking, erasure or destruction of personal information relating to them on the basis that it is inaccurate. This right is enforceable through the Courts. The Court may also choose to require the data controller's records (and those of any other data controllers holding the same data) to be supplemented with data recording the true facts as approved by the Court.

EXAMPLES OF BREACHES OF SUBJECT RIGHTS

The first example below illustrates the real concern of individuals who feel that they may have been disadvantaged by an unsatisfactory reference given in confidence. It is particularly pertinent in relation to financial services, where a high degree of disclosure in references is required to meet the regulator's requirements for 'approved persons'. The individual in this case was concerned that the situation could recur if the problem was not addressed.

An individual complained that soon after starting a new job he was dismissed by his employer due to a personal reference his employer believed was unsatisfactory. The complainant requested a copy of the reference under section 7 of the Act, in order to assess the accuracy of its contents. In addition, the individual was concerned that unless he was able to see the reference, he would have difficulty in finding new employment as he would be unsure of being able to supply good references in future. The individual's employer refused to release the document in question on grounds of confidentiality. The Information Commissioner contacted the employer and explained the various factors an employer should consider when in receipt of a subject access request that includes information relating to a third party. After considering this advice, the employer agreed to release an edited version of the references to the individual. The identity of the third party was withheld.

In a case quoted on the Information Commissioner's website in 2001,[5] an NHS Trust repeatedly failed to meet the 40-day target for dealing with subject access requests. The difficulties it was experiencing related to the inclusion of accessible health records, which meant providing copies of X-rays. The Information Commissioner had received a number of complaints and requests for assessment about this NHS Trust so a compliance visit was carried out. Improvements to their administrative arrangements were agreed to ensure that in future the subject access requirements would be met.

---

5   Information Commissioner (2001) *Annual Report Summary for 2001*, p. 5. Available from www.informationcommisioner.gov.uk.

This case is interesting because it highlights a trend for patients pursuing a personal injury claim to request copies of their X-rays to support their claim. The high cost of obtaining copies of X-rays is being avoided by using data protection law and exercising the subject right of access. Solicitors involved in personal injury claims are presumably advising their clients to obtain expensive information in this much cheaper way. Note that the view of the Information Commissioner did not include reference to this reason why individuals were making so many enquiries involving copies of X-rays. An organisation cannot decline to respond to a subject access request on the grounds of the proposed use of the information supplied. Since this decision, the circumstances in which copies of accessible health records can be requested have been revised. Also it is now permissible for NHS Trusts to charge up to £50 for providing copies of documents such as X-rays in permanent form.

CONCLUSION

The challenges in responding to the exercise of rights under the Act are twofold: first, identifying when a statutory right is being exercised and second, meeting the statutory deadlines for dealing with it. Regular staff training is the only way to ensure that potential data protection implications of incoming requests for information or complaints are identified. Very rarely will members of the public know that they are exercising a right under the Act so staff must be familiar with the range of rights and have considered the form that notices to exercise them might take.

Timely identification of a subject right is the essential first step in dealing with the issue within the prescribed time limits. Where there are specific time limits, for example, for dealing with the right of subject access, these are absolute even if compliance is to the financial detriment of the organisation.

CHAPTER 19

Outsourcing to India

Increasingly, organisations compare the cost of undertaking specific functions within the organisation with the cost of outsourcing to an external service provider to perform that function on its behalf. The availability of skills to carry out a particular function may also be a significant factor, but labour costs and the cost of property are usually the prime motive. Currently, there is a significant trend towards outsourcing administrative functions to India, where a large, skilled and educated workforce is available at lower cost than would be available in the UK.

Outsourcing work involving personal data processing on any scale, that is placing work with third parties to carry out tasks on behalf of the organisation in return for remuneration, is now subject to a new statutory duty under the seventh data protection principle. The new requirement entails checking the service provider complies with appropriate organisational and technical security measures to ensure the security of the information it processes to the same standard as the organisation outsourcing the work. It also involves incorporating two terms in written contracts with service suppliers to deal with specific data protection issues relating to control of the information being processed.

Outsourcing work to a third party located outside the EEA involves a data transfer that is subject to the eighth data protection principle, which restricts such transfers unless there is adequate security for the information to be transferred.

Both of these issues, outsourcing and using a service provider located outside the EEA, involve additional compliance measures if the organisation is to meet its obligations under data protection law. This chapter considers the requirements and what may be done to meet them.

THE EFFECT OF THE SEVENTH PRINCIPLE

The seventh principle aims to regulate the relationship between organisations and third-party service providers involved in processing personal information on their behalf (data processors). Its application is quite specific. The definition in section 1(1) of the Data Protection Act 1998 (the Act) states that a data processor, 'in relation to personal data, means any person (other than an employee of the data controller) who processes the data on behalf of the data controller'.

Not all outsource service providers fall within the definition of a 'data processor'; it depends on the circumstances. However, if personal information is being processed by a third party on behalf of the organisation, the relationship between the organisation and the third party is one to which the seventh principle might apply and further investigation is warranted.

IDENTIFYING DATA PROCESSORS

A key point is that a data processor is a third party and is independent of the organisation, although it might be another company in the same group. A data processor might be described as the agent of the organisation. Deciding whether or not a third party is a data processor is a matter of fact, but it will be a provider of a service in which it has no interest except the payment it receives for carrying out the work.

The answers to the following questions will help a data controller to decide whether or not a party is a data processor.

- *Does one party process on the instructions of the other?*
  If the organisation is the decision maker as regards the purposes for which personal data will be processed, it is likely to be the data controller. If it acts only on instructions, it will be a data processor.

- *Does the service provider process personal information supplied by or on behalf of the organisation?*
  For example, a company might buy a mailing list from a third party and arrange for the list containing personal information to be supplied direct to its preferred mailing house. Although the personal information is not supplied directly by the data controller, it is supplied on its behalf. This does not affect the underlying relationship between mailing house and the company. The mailing house is a data processor on behalf of the company.

- *Is processing undertaken on behalf of the organisation?*
  Processing undertaken on behalf of the organisation indicates that the service provider is a data processor.

- *Does the service provider have any interest in the personal information it processes apart from remuneration for the service provided to the organisation?*
  If there is any indication of an interest in the information, perhaps a joint marketing approach, then it is likely that the parties are joint data controllers.

- *Does the service provider take decisions in regard to the personal information it processes?*

  The processor may be a data controller in its own right if it uses the personal information for its own purposes or deals with it in any way that would suggest that it is the data controller.

- *What do the parties intend should happen to the files containing personal information when the relationship between them ends?*

  If the service provider is a data processor, personal data will either be returned to the data controller or its nominated representative, or deleted. The data processor will have no further use for the information.

A service company within a trading group may be a data processor. Data protection law does not recognise trading groups of companies. Each corporate entity is viewed as a separate data controller and all other corporate entities are 'third parties' despite issues of ownership in common or branding.

When organisations set up separate corporate entities on a functional basis, this can create anomalies and paradoxes. It may be reasonable for a large business to set up separate subsidiaries, for example, for HR or information technology, and delegate authority and responsibility on a group-wide basis to those companies. However, the trading companies remain the data controllers, at least in relation to customers, and therefore are obliged to:

- Have written contracts between themselves and the functional subsidiary companies.

- Monitor the activity of those companies.

As a consequence, when staff are employed by a service company but they actually carry out functions on behalf of the trading companies, the service company is a data processor and the trading companies are data controllers for purposes of the seventh principle.

COMPLIANCE ACTIVITY

When inviting tenders for outsourced work, service providers should be asked about their policy on data protection and for details of their relevant security arrangements. On the new appointment of a service provider, the specific terms laid down by the seventh principle should be incorporated into the contract between the organisation and the service provider.

Existing arrangements with service providers should be checked to identify those that involve the processing of personal information on behalf of the organisation.

Then the required contract terms should be incorporated into the existing contractual arrangements either by drawing up new contracts, or by exchange of side letters. At review meetings, or from time to time by letter, the organisation should ask about security arrangements and investigate any breaches of security, in order to meet its statutory obligations.

Queries to raise with existing and prospective service providers

Identifying data processors is not always clear cut and it may be better if the parties try to reach agreement as to their respective roles and obligations. Service providers should be advised that the relationship with the organisation appears to be one involving the service provider in processing personal information on behalf of the organisation. If this is the case, the seventh principle will apply to the relationship. The service provider should be given an opportunity to agree or disagree with the assessment.

If the service provider is unaware of the implications of the seventh principle, it should be explained that the Act places certain statutory duties on the organisation to check the ongoing security arrangements of service providers. Useful information to be provided by the service provider would include:

- a statement of compliance with current data protection law;

- such details of the service provider's security arrangements as it is able to provide without compromising security;

- details as to how new employees are monitored;

- the controls within which new employees work to ensure that the service provider is satisfied as to their reliability;

- confirmation that appropriate procedures are in place relating to the exercise of subject rights;

- confirmation that all staff are given training on how to handle the exercise of subject rights;

- confirmation that the service provider will advise the organisation immediately should any data subject of personal information processed on its behalf exercise their subject rights.

FSA REPORT INTO OUTSOURCING TO INDIA

In 2005, the FSA published its findings from an enquiry into the security aspects of outsourcing to India.[1] It visited ten operations in India and obtained input from five

---

1   Financial Services Authority (2005) *Offshore Operations: Industry Feedback*. Available from www.fsa.gov.uk/ pubs/other/offshore_ops.pdf.

others as well as visiting firms in the UK before and after visiting India to gain an insight into governance and control mechanisms in place. In its report 'Offshore Operations: Industry Feedback', it concludes that risk management and governance frameworks are adequate and in place; however, it identified risks in the areas of prevention of financial crime and consumer protection.

The overall conclusion reached by the FSA was that offshoring can contribute a material risk to FSA objectives for market confidence, reduction of financial crime and consumer protection. It expressed concerns that service users would experience difficulties in monitoring and controlling outsourced operations at such a distance. In general, it found that the firms interviewed were aware of the risks and problems and had introduced measures to counter them. By definition, the firms involved in the review were major groups and the FSA expected them to have appropriate risk management control frameworks in place. It commented that 'any firm undertaking this sort of activity would need to be able to demonstrate appropriate oversight from the UK'.

The FSA's concerns for the fledgling industry in India were staff attrition and business continuity planning.

CONTRACT TERMS

It is also a requirement of the Act that specific clauses be introduced to the contract between organisations and their service providers. Suggested wording for the clauses is set out below.

In addition to the clauses required by statute, a couple of additional clauses may be usefully included. The first is to require the data processor to ensure that it passes on these obligations to any contractors, sub-contractors or outsource service suppliers it might use. The second is to require that any information reasonably requested by the organisation will be supplied. This should enable regular checks on security arrangements to be undertaken. For example, if the service provider is regulated, the organisation might want to view any audit reports made by the regulator into the service provider's business.

Suggested terms for inclusion in the contract

To the extent that [the service provider] is a data processor within the meaning of the Data Protection Act 1998 it hereby undertakes:

only to act on instructions from [client] when processing personal data on its behalf

> *to comply with the 7th Data Protection Principle in relation to the processing of personal data on [client's] behalf*
>
> *to ensure that equivalent obligations of security are imposed on any third party service supplier to [the service provider] ('subcontractors') which process personal data on behalf of the [client]*
>
> *to report on security issues as may be required by the [client] from time to time.*

DATA PROCESSORS OUTSIDE OF UK JURISDICTION

Where a data processor is located outside the EEA, the seventh principle still applies and the organisation must check for compliance with appropriate security measures and put a written contract in place as described above. The data processor may be outside the jurisdiction of the Act, but the organisation within the jurisdiction must ensure that its data processor adheres to security requirements commensurate with those required by the seventh principle regardless of its geographic location.

When selecting a data processor located outside of the EEA, consideration must be given to the eighth principle, which restricts the transfer of personal information outside the EEA. The key points of the restriction are:

- there is a prohibition on the transfer of personal information;

- outside the EEA;

- unless there is an adequate level of protection for the rights and freedoms of data subjects.

A transfer to an outsource service provider located in a third country (that is one not within the EEA) must be authorised by reference to one of the following:

- an EC decision as to adequacy;

- a prescribed condition to authorise the transfer;

- appropriate contract terms in the form approved by the EC;

- an assessment of adequacy.

This issue is considered in depth in Chapter 11 on the eighth principle. What follows is a summary of the key points.

EC DECISIONS AS TO ADEQUACY

Third countries with a high standard of data protection within their jurisdiction can apply to the EC for a decision as to adequacy. To date the following countries have had a successful assessment made: Argentina, Canada, Guernsey, Isle of Man and Switzerland. Transfers of personal data to organisations located in any of these territories are not subject to the restriction but are made freely.

In addition, in the USA, companies that subscribe to Safe Harbor are deemed to offer adequate security; although the USA is not an approved destination, individual companies may be so.

PRESCRIBED CONDITIONS

The key condition to legitimise a transfer of personal data to a third country is where the transfer is necessary pursuant to a contract with the individual concerned. This will cover many situations where personal data is transferred to a parent company located outside the EEA – to authorise a contract or terms of employment, for example.

Another key qualifying condition is where the transfer is made with the consent of the individual concerned. This does raise the usual issues with consent. An organisation that relies on consent must be able to handle those cases where the individual withholds or revokes consent. The Information Commissioner has suggested that consent should only be considered when alternative options have been exhausted and it is particularly unreliable in the context of employment where the argument that the employer automatically brings undue influence on the individual employee to give their consent is difficult to counter.

TRANSFER ON APPROPRIATE CONTRACT TERMS

Another key condition for authorising transfers of personal data to countries located outside the EEA is where the transfer is made on approved contract terms. The terms have to have been approved by the EC and the first set of terms were approved and published in 2001. Practitioners and corporate entities alike have reported problems with the terms being too prescriptive and inflexible. In January 2005, the EC announced that it was working on new standard contractual clauses so that personal data can be transferred from an organisation located in the EEA to a data processor established in a third country.

THE ASSESSMENT OF ADEQUACY

If none of the conditions apply[2] and the country of the intended transfer of the personal data has not been presumed adequate by the EC, the organisation is required to make its own assessment of adequacy. The adequacy of protection for data subjects' rights and freedoms in relation to data protection must be made both in respect of the territory where the transferee is located and as offered by the transferee organisation. It is important to note that each separate transfer of personal information must go through the adequacy assessment. The organisation cannot assume adequacy for future transfers based on its assessment of adequacy for a current transfer. Given that many outsourced services are of a continuing nature, the inappropriateness of the adequacy assessment route to legitimise regular data transfers is apparent.

Certain circumstances may help to establish adequacy where the transfer is one between a data controller and its data processor. Where an appropriate contract is in place to meet the requirements of the seventh principle, this goes a significant way towards establishing adequacy. However, the Information Commissioner has stated that organisations cannot rely on this alone.[3]

The factors to consider when making an assessment of adequacy are:

- the nature of the personal information;

- the country or territory of origin of the information contained in the information;

- the country or territory of final destination of that information;

- the purposes for which and period during which the information is intended to be processed;

- the law in force in the country or territory in question;

- the international obligations of that country or territory;

- any relevant codes of conduct or other rules that are enforceable in that country or territory (whether generally or by arrangement in particular cases);

- any security measures taken in respect of the information in that country or territory.[4]

The Information Commissioner has published guidance on how to carry out an adequacy assessment and has recommended a 'good practice' approach, as follows:

---

2   There are more conditions set out in the Data Protection Act 1998, Schedule 4 and considered in Chapter 11.
3   *Transborder Dataflows*, para. 11.5.
4   The Data Protection Act 1998, Schedule 1, Part II, para. 13.

1. Consider the type of transfer involved and whether this assists in determining adequacy; for example if the transfer is within an industry sector where professional rules or standards apply (underwriters for example) or is a transfer within an international group of companies. Although this will not establish adequacy prima facie, it may go some way towards it because the data controller has a level of knowledge about the security and procedures within the transferee company and may have an on-going relationship that both parties will wish to protect.

2. Consider:

    –   The nature of the personal information (take care with sensitive data in particular).

    –   The country or territory of origin of the personal information. It may not have originated within the EEA where higher data protection standards apply; if it originated outside the EEA, what level of data protection do the subjects ordinarily enjoy?

    –   The purposes for which and period during which the information is intended to be processed.

    –   The harm that might result from improper processing.

    –   The law in force in the country or territory in question.

    –   The international obligations of that country or territory.

    –   Any relevant codes of conduct or other rules that are enforceable in the country or territory.

    –   Any security measures taken in respect of the data in that country or territory.

    –   The extent to which data protection standards have been adopted.

    –   Whether there is a means of ensuring the standards are achieved in practice.

    –   Whether there is an effective mechanism for individuals to enforce their rights or obtain redress if things go wrong.

3. Identify any circumstances in the knowledge of the organisation, or of others involved in the proposed transfer, that put it on notice that it is not appropriate to make the transfer; for example if the organisation is aware of breaches of confidentiality at the transferee company or other information security problems.

As a matter of principle, there are three issues with the adequacy test. First, the prospective transferor takes full responsibility when deciding whether or not the third country offers an adequate level of protection for data transferred. The final decision will be subjective and there is every possibility that it will be made by a designated individual, putting significant pressure onto that individual. Second, it is a critical decision and, if undertaken properly, will utilise key resources in assessing the circumstances of the proposed transfer equating to time and cost. Finally, the assessment of adequacy is an inappropriate route for organisations wishing either to transfer personal information simultaneously to a large number of organisations located in third countries or to make regular transfers of personal information to organisations located in third countries. The adequacy test is basically a method of authorising one-off transfers of information.

CONCLUSION

To meet the specific requirements in relation to outsourced functions, organisations should identify their existing data processors and those circumstances where a data controller to data processor relationship is likely to arise. In the latter cases and when existing contracts are put out to tender, the selection process should include careful vetting of prospective data processors to check that system and organisational security measures are adequate. There is a significant overlap with business requirements in this respect, organisations normally require an appropriate degree of security and confidentiality from outsource service providers regardless of the requirements of the Act. The key to compliance is, as ever, to document the checks carried out.

Written contracts are required with all data processors. The terms of the contract must include requirements that the data processor act only on the instructions of the data controller in relation to processing personal data and that it adhere to the seventh data protection principle. The organisation's legal department should determine whether the relationship is one to which the seventh principle applies and to insert the required wording as necessary.

On a continuing basis, the data controller should monitor the performance of its data processors in relation to security. Any reported breaches of security should be investigated with emphasis on preventing the problem from recurring.

Where an outsource service provider is located in a third country, the organisation also needs to take action to ensure that the transfer of personal information to its data processor can be authorised so that it does not breach the eighth principle. There are several applicable conditions and circumstances in which transfers of personal information outside the EEA are justified. The adequacy assessment is such that it applies to individual, one-off, transfers of information. It cannot legitimise transfers in a continuing relationship. This makes it an inappropriate vehicle for authorising transfers to a data processor located in a third country. Alternative solutions, such as making transfers on approved contract terms, should be investigated.

PART III

The Regulatory Framework

This part of the book considers the issues that relate to regulation in the UK. Chapter 20 considers the role of the Information Commissioner, the regulatory authority for data protection, and Chapter 21 discusses notification (or registration for data protection as it was called prior to the implementation of the Data Protection Act 1998). Chapter 22 discusses criminal offences under the Data Protection Act 1998, as these describe the regulatory environment relevant to data protection.

In addition, as no book that purports to deal with the data protection issues facing organisations in the financial services sector can ignore the impact of financial regulation Chapter 23 on the FSA covers issues such as whistle blowing and the disclosure of information to and by the regulator.

Finally, Chapter 24 considers the impact of potentially conflicting laws and regulations.

CHAPTER 20

The Information Commissioner

The role of the Data Protection Registrar was created by the Data Protection Act 1984. The Registrar's Office was set up to be an independent regulatory authority and that remains the case. The Information Commissioner is an independent official appointed by the Crown, reporting annually to parliament.

The EC Directive on Data Protection (95/46/EC) was published in final form in 1995. It was intended to harmonise data protection regulation throughout the member states of the EU. A deadline for national law to implement its provisions was set for October 1998. The Data Protection Act 1998 was the instrument to implement the EC Directive in the UK. Most EC member states have now brought in appropriate legislation. One of the requirements of the EC Directive was that member states should appoint a Data Protection Commissioner, so the 1998 Act changed the name of the Data Protection Registrar to that of Data Protection Commissioner. With the introduction of the Freedom of Information Act 2000 in the UK, the name changed again, to that of Information Commissioner.

The mission statement of the Office of the Information Commissioner is as follows:[1]

Promoting public access to official information and protecting your personal information.

STRUCTURE OF THE OFFICE OF THE INFORMATION COMMISSIONER

The Information Commissioner is supported by a team of approximately 130 staff in the following departments:

- Strategic Policy Group, which develops data protection guidance;

- Freedom of Information group;

- Compliance Department, which includes an enquiry line;

---

1   Taken from the website of the Information Commissioner, www.informationcommissioner.gov.uk.

- Legal Department;

- Investigations Department;

- Notification Department, responsible for maintaining the Register of Data Controllers;

- Marketing Department.

There are three recently created posts of Assistant Commissioner. The Assistant Commissioners carry specific remits for data protection in Northern Ireland, Scotland and Wales and freedom of information in Northern Ireland and Wales. They also contribute to the formulation of key policy and service delivery across the UK. Scotland has its own Information Commissioner for Freedom of Information.

RESPONSIBILITIES AND FUNCTIONS

The responsibilities and functions of the Information Commissioner in relation to data protection are set out in the Data Protection Act 1998 (the Act).[2] In general terms these are:

- a duty to promote awareness of data protection and good practice by data controllers;

- a duty to provide information to the public about the Act and any relevant developments in data protection law arising in the EC;

- a duty to develop codes of practice and to encourage trade associations and bodies to do likewise;

- a duty to carry out assessments (investigation of complaints);

- the duty to maintain a register of notifications made by data controllers.[3]

As the designated authority in the UK for international cooperation on data protection matters, the Information Commissioner is:

- the supervisory authority in the UK for the purposes of the EC Directive on Data Protection;

- the point of contact for international initiatives on data protection;

- the conduit for communication with the EC and EU member states on matters pertaining to data protection.

---

2   The Data Protection Act 1998, Part VI.
3   This duty is set out in the Data Protection Act 1998, section 19.

The current (2005) Information Commissioner sees his objectives as:[4]

● challenging traditional cultures of unnecessary secrecy across the public sector;

● ensuring a culture of respect for personal information;

● balancing open government and privacy against other public interests;

● helping organisations to achieve compliance with the Data Protection Act and the Freedom of Information Act;

● fostering an environment where freedom of information and data protection are a natural way of life.

PROMOTING AWARENESS AND ISSUING GUIDANCE

The Information Commissioner has a duty to promote the development and use of codes of practice. Codes of practice may be European or specific to the UK. There is a working party (the Article 29 Working Party) that considers codes of practice and proposed codes at the European level. In June 2003, the Article 29 Working Party approved the European code of conduct of FEDMA[5] for the use of personal information in direct marketing. It concluded that the code is in accordance with the provisions of the EC Directive[6] and that it added value to the EC Directive by applying its provisions to the specific issues of the direct marketing industry.

At UK level, several codes of practice have been drafted by trade associations with input from the Information Commissioner's Office. The Press Complaints Commission's 2005 guidance note on the Act and journalism was produced with the input from the Information Commissioner.[7] Other codes have been produced by the Information Commissioner, such as the *Employment Practices Data Protection Code*, published in sections between 2000 and 2004, and the *CCTV Code of Practice*, published in July 2000.

The Information Commissioner's Office is also responsible for raising awareness of data protection issues and publishing guidance for industry, the public sector and consumers. Examples include:

● *Legal Guidance* on the Act published in December 2001;

---

4   Taken from the Information Commissioner's website, www.informationcommissioner.gov.uk.
5   Federation of European Direct Marketing.
6   EC Directive 95/46/EC.
7   Press Complaints Commission (2005) *Data Protection Act, Journalism and the PCC Code.* Available from www.pcc.org.uk.

- *Guide to Data Protection Auditing*, issued in December 2001;

- educational CD-ROM *The Plumstones*, for use in schools, issued in September 2002;

- publication of a comicbook-style guide *How to manage your personal information under the Data Protection Act* in June 2004;

- guidance on cold calling regulation, *Corporate Registration on TPS*, published in May 2004.

CARRYING OUT ASSESSMENTS AND ENFORCEMENT ACTIVITY

An assessment is an investigation of the circumstances of processing activity carried out at the request of an individual or organisation (not necessarily a data subject of the organisation under investigation). At the end of the investigation, the Information Commissioner's Office will issue its formal assessment of the compliance or non-compliance of the activity complained of and any data subject who believes that they have been disadvantaged by the processing is at liberty to take the matter up in the civil courts. Assessments are not necessarily linked to legal enforcement action.

Organisations can be compelled to cooperate with an assessment. If the Information Commissioner's Office requests information to facilitate the assessment and the organisation fails or refuses to comply, it has a power under section 43 of the Act to require the information to be provided. Failure to comply with such a notice is a criminal offence.[8]

Assessments are handled separately from enforcement activity. Generally, the enforcement procedure is only followed after communication has failed to persuade a data controller to amend its personal information processing activities. There are signs that the Information Commissioner's Office is starting to take a tougher line with enforcement and that specific problems are being addressed. In 2001–02, the Baird Project targeted the unlawful obtaining of personal information from the Inland Revenue and the Department of Work and Pensions by organisations such as private investigators. A number of cases were brought to trial and successfully prosecuted arising from the project.

June 2005 saw the introduction of a new division within the Information Commissioner's Office. The new 'Regulatory Action Division' will handle complaints previously handled by the Compliance Team.

---

8   The Data Protection Act 1998, section 47.

Where a data controller fails to amend its personal information processing activities despite pressure from the Information Commissioner's Office to adopt compliant strategies, the enforcement procedure culminates in the issue of an enforcement notice that sets out the steps that the organisation is required to take. Failure to comply with an enforcement notice is a criminal offence and the final sanction of the Information Commissioner's Office is to bring criminal charges.[9] Organisations have a right of appeal to the Information Tribunal, a body that considers enforcements and decision notices issued by the Information Commissioner. However, the stated approach of the Information Commissioner's Office is to use enforcement as a last resort.

---

9   The Data Protection Act 1998, section 47.

CHAPTER 21

Notification

The Data Protection Act 1984 introduced the requirement for organisations and individuals involved in certain industries to register for data protection purposes. Registration is now known as 'notification' in accordance with the EC Directive on Data Protection.[1]

ACTIVITIES SUBJECT TO NOTIFICATION

Under the Data Protection Act 1998 (the Act), all data controllers are required to notify unless they are exempt.[2] The exemptions are set out in The Data Protection (Notification and Notification Fees) Regulations 2000 as amended. Most, if not all, organisations involved in financial services activities are required to notify for data protection purposes, as the exemptions apply to smaller businesses that do not process personal information except in relation to their staff and to administer client accounts. Any organisation that processes personal information as part of its key service offering, such as pensions administration, consulting and insurance administration is not within the terms of the exemption. Here is a list of some financial services activities ('purposes of processing' in the terminology of notification) that are notifiable:

- **Credit referencing:** *The provision of information relating to the financial status of individuals or organisations on behalf of other organisations. This purpose is for use by credit reference agencies, not for organisations who merely contact or use credit reference agencies.*

- **Debt administration and factoring:** *The tracing of consumer and commercial debtors and the collection on behalf of creditors. The purchasing of consumer or trade debts, including rentals and instalment credit payments, from businesses.*

- **Health administration and services:** *The provision and administration of patient care.*

- **Insurance administration:** *The administration of life, health, pensions, property, motor and other insurance business. This applies only to insurance*

---

1   EC Directive 95/46/EC.
2   The Data Protection Act 1998, section 19.

companies doing risk assessments, payment of claims and underwriting. Insurance consultants and intermediaries should use the purpose described as 'provision of financial services and advice'.

- **Pensions administration:** *The administration of funded pensions or superannuation schemes. Data controllers using this purpose will usually be the trustees or administrators of pension funds.*

- **Provision of financial services and advice:** *The provision of services as an intermediary in respect of any financial transactions including mortgage and insurance broking.*

The following arrangements also require organisations to notify, even if the exemptions would otherwise have applied:

- Complex organisations involving groups of companies that 'share' personal information. This includes corporate groups where there is a service or employing company and one or more trading companies. The normal operation of the business requires that personal information is shared between the employing company and the trading company(ies) for work planning and management.

- The operation of a CCTV scheme.

- The use of credit reference information.

- Sharing trade and personal information.

- Marketing goods and services using personal information obtained from a third party (that is, buying or renting mailing lists or undertaking joint promotions with other companies to their customers).

- Marketing goods and services on behalf of third parties or clients.

EXEMPTIONS

There is a small business exemption or 'core business exemption' that applies where the organisation is not involved in any of the above activities. It applies to those organisations that only process personal information for:

- advertising, marketing and PR only in relation to its own goods and services;

- administration of customer/client and supplier records;

- staff administration.

Another exemption from notification applies to organisations that do not process personal information on computer or word processor, but that hold records only in paper files.

There is a further exemption for charitable organisations. It applies where the data controller is a not-for-profit organisation and processes personal information only to establish and maintain membership records and records of those with whom it has regular contact. The exemption also allows administration of employees, accounts and record-keeping, and limited advertising and promotional activity directed solely towards its own members.

In all cases, it must be stressed that exemption from notification in no way reduces the obligation on the organisation to comply with provisions of the Act.

WHO CAN NOTIFY?

Legal persons and real persons may notify, as may unincorporated associations. The requirement is for companies to register as distinct legal entities, although a group of companies may register under a brand name as an unincorporated association in addition if that is appropriate.

CONSEQUENCES OF NOT BEING REGISTERED

Under section 17 of the Act, processing of personal information is prohibited if the organisation should be registered and is not so registered. Further, it is a criminal offence under section 21 of the Act to fail to notify if required to do so. Note that this is a strict liability offence, which means that there are no defences. If business activities do not fall within the exemptions from notification, the business needs to be registered.

Any changes in activities must also be notified to the Data Protection Register; again failure to do so is a criminal offence.[3]

HOW TO NOTIFY

Notification can be instigated by telephone or online. Entries on the register are based on a standard template for each industry, so it is important to check that it covers all of the organisation's personal information processing activities.

---

3   The Data Protection Act 1998, section 21.

RISK MANAGEMENT STRATEGIES

Notification entries should be checked regularly against personal information processing activities to pick up those changes to activities that might be notifiable. This is another area where regular, independent audit is invaluable. Organisations involved in 'brand-stretch'[4] activities, acquisitions, takeovers and de-mergers are likely to find that personal information processing activities change over time. It is all too easy to fail to keep register entries up to date. In addition, the format required for notification has changed since the 1984 Data Protection Act was introduced and guidance and interpretation of regulations has evolved, potentially leaving data controllers stranded when the rest of the industry has moved on. A useful audit tip is to check out the registration entries of competitors from time to time to check that the organisation has not been left behind in the latest developments on notification.

CONCLUSION

The notification process has been streamlined and simplified since its introduction under the Data Protection Act 1984 and businesses should not find it a barrier to registration in itself. Neither are the costs prohibitively high. Therefore, given that failure to notify when required to do so is a strict liability offence, common sense would dictate that it is better to notify if there is any doubt as to whether an exemption applies to current processing activity.

---

4   'Brand-stretch' refers to taking a well-known brand in relation to one service or set of goods and applying the brand to a new area of operations. An example is when high-street retailers and supermarkets move into financial products by offering store credit cards, loans, deposits and insurance.

CHAPTER 22

Criminal Offences

There are a number of criminal offences created by the Data Protection Act 1998 (the Act) and one recently introduced under the Freedom of Information Act 2000 (FOI) that applies only to public bodies as defined by FOI.

NOTIFICATION OFFENCES

Notification is the term for registration in accordance with the requirement of the EC Directive on Data Protection.[1] Section 17 of the Act places a prohibition on the processing of personal information unless the data controller is registered and section 21 then applies to make it a criminal offence to fail to register when processing activities involve personal information. The previous chapter explained the notification requirements in more detail but, in summary, section 21 creates a 'strict liability' offence, which means that there are no defences to it. If the organisation is not exempt from notification (there are limited exemptions) it should notify and if it fails to do so, it has committed a criminal offence.

In addition, section 20 of the Act requires data controllers to notify changes to their personal information processing activities. Again, pursuant to section 21, it is a criminal offence to fail to keep the notification up to date with current personal information processing activity. However, in this case, it is a defence if the person charged with the offence can show that they exercised all due diligence to comply with the requirement to keep the notification up to date and accurate.

UNAUTHORISED DISCLOSURE AND OBTAINING

Section 55 of the Act makes it a criminal offence to knowingly or recklessly obtain or disclose personal information without the consent of the data controller. If the data controller obtains or discloses personal information outside of its authority to process (based on subject information and its Data Protection Register entry) it will be in breach of the first and/or second data protection principles. However, where individuals, perhaps employees, act outside of their authority from the organisation, then a criminal offence has been committed.

---

1   EC Directive 46/95/EC, Article 18.

The offence is frequently reported in relation to police officers using their access to DVLA and other records for personal reasons. In a case during 2004, a computer operator working for a police force in Wales used her position to access police records relating to her friends, not out of malice, but simply out of curiosity.[2] She was found guilty by magistrates of four charges contrary to the Act, section 55, knowingly or recklessly obtaining personal information without the consent of the data controller.

The offence is also reported in relation to private investigators and tracing agents who falsely represent themselves as data subjects to gain access to personal information held on government agency files. The Information Commissioner ran a joint initiative with the Department for Work and Pensions and the Inland Revenue, the Baird Project, whose objective was to identify persons and organisations that systematically use unlawful means to obtain personal details from those government agencies with a view to selling the information on to clients. The Baird Project concluded in March 2002 and a number of cases were brought to trial and successfully prosecuted arising from the project.

ENFORCED SUBJECT ACCESS

Since the introduction of the Criminal Records Bureau, which allows certain categories of employer to apply for details of an individual's criminal record, if any, it has been an offence under section 56 of the Act to require candidates for employment to apply to the police for a copy of their criminal record using the right of subject access.

The Criminal Records Bureau is now the only legal way to check whether or not an individual has a criminal record and checks may only be carried out in respect of people who work with children and certain other vulnerable groups.

FRUSTRATING A SUBJECT ACCESS REQUEST

The FOI introduces a new offence of destroying records in order to frustrate a subject access request or a request made under the FOI.[3] Any public authority employee who deletes or destroys records in order to frustrate a subject access request could be guilty of the offence.

---

2   Reported on 6 July 2004 in the *Western Mail*. Available from icwales.icnetwork.co.uk/0100news/0200wales.
3   The Freedom of Information Act 2000, section 77, brought into force by The Freedom of Information Act 2000 (Commencement No. 4) Order 2004.

LIABILITY FOR DATA PROTECTION OFFENCES

Companies can be guilty of the offences in the Act, such as failure to notify and the failure to keep its notification up to date.

A director, manager or officer of a company can be liable for Data Protection Act offences[4] if they consent to, or connive at, the commission of the offence or if the offence can be shown to be attributable to any neglect on their part.

Data protection law is unusual in that there are criminal sanctions against individual employees too, not just against the company and its directors. Offences under the Act may be committed by individuals, such as unauthorised disclosure or obtaining of personal information.

The *Employment Practices Data Protection Code*[5] stresses the duty of the employer to undertake staff training to highlight data protection issues and the risk of personal liability to those staff whose work involves handling personal information. Where an individual employee is found guilty of an offence, the employer must show that employees had been trained about unauthorised disclosures and other misuse of personal information if it is to avoid a charge that it had been negligent.

PENALTIES

On summary conviction, the limit is a £5000 fine; on indictment it is unlimited. However, it is possible for the court to apply the fine in respect of each offence committed where a number of offences have taken place. In a recent court case,[6] an accountant was found guilty under section 55 of the Act of unlawful obtaining and/or disclosure of personal information. The accountant had been an agent for Bradford & Bingley building society and, as such, had introduced a number of clients to the building society. When the building society terminated its agency agreement with the accountant, he contacted clients and advised them to close their building society accounts and open new ones with a bank where he had a new agency agreement in place. The accountant admitted a number of other similar offences and was fined £10 000 in total.

---

4   The Data Protection Act 1998, section 61.
5   Available from www.informationcommissioner.gov.uk/cms/DocumentUploads/ICO_EmpPracCode.pdf.
6   Press release dated 23 October 2003. Available from www.informationcommissioner.gov.uk.

CHAPTER 23

The Financial Services Authority

This chapter considers the impact of the FSA on data protection regulation. It does not seek to be a reference for other queries and issues relating to the FSA. As with Chapter 24 on the conflict of laws and regulation, this chapter seeks to highlight the general issues that arise when different influences are brought to bear on a piece of legislation.

Regulation necessitates the flow of information from regulated organisations to the regulator. In its turn, the regulator may put information into the public domain or disclose it to other regulatory bodies, such as the Inland Revenue for example. In its operations, the FSA is itself subject to data protection law, as it carries out these duties and they in turn give rise to specific data protection issues. These are the issues considered in this chapter.

ABOUT THE FSA

The FSA is an independent regulatory organisation, given statutory powers by the Financial Services and Markets Act 2000 (FSMA). It is financed by levies on organisations in the financial services industry. Its board of directors is appointed by the Treasury.

The FSA regulates the financial services industry in the UK. It has four statutory objectives:[1]

- maintaining confidence in the financial system

- promoting public understanding of the financial system

- securing the appropriate degree of protection for consumers

- reducing financial crime.

Primarily, the FSA is engaged in the authorisation and supervision of banks, building societies, insurance companies, insurance brokers, investment firms, markets and

---

1   Financial Services and Markets Act 2000, sections 3 to 6 inclusive.

exchanges, including Lloyds. It is the listing authority for public listed companies in the UK.

THE USE OF PERSONAL INFORMATION BY THE FSA

The FSA has published a statement on its activities and powers in relation to the use of personal information 'The Protection of Regulatory Information under English Law' dated March 2004.[2] The statement summarises how English law protects information obtained by the FSA under the FSMA in sections 348 and 349 and regulations made by HM Treasury.

When carrying out its duties as a regulator, the FSA is exempt from many of the requirements of the Data Protection Act 1998 (the Act). Certain bodies and functions, the FSA among them, are required to publish information. The FSA is required to publish details relating to 'approved persons' and 'appointed representatives'. Where this involves the publication of personal information, for example where an approved person is a living individual, there is an exemption in the Act to allow for the publication of information required by statute. The FSA duty to publish information overrides data protection considerations in relation to personal information and the statutory duty to publish takes precedence.[3]

In its privacy statement, the regulator draws attention to this as follows:

> be aware that any personal details that are provided on ... forms, including signatures, will be placed onto the public file of the society to which the application or notification relates.

> This means any personal details disclosed on such forms will be available to anyone who asks the FSA for access to the society's public record file.

DISCLOSURES REQUIRED BY LAW

In carrying out its duties as a regulator, the FSA requires organisations to provide it with certain information that may include personal information. This constitutes a disclosure by the organisation that ordinarily it would seek to authorise by reference to its entry on the Data Protection Register and by reference to subject information (an explanation about the organisation and the purposes to which personal information will be put) provided to the individual to whom the personal information relates.

---

2   Financial Services Authority (2004) *The Protection of Regulatory Information under English Law*. Available from www.fsa.gov.uk.
3   The Data Protection Act 1998, section 34.

However, the Act incorporates certain exemptions that apply to legal and regulatory activity. There is a key exemption from non-disclosure provisions where disclosure is required by statute or by any rule of law or by the order of a court.[4] In this context the 'non-disclosure provisions' are the first data protection principle requiring fair and lawful processing and provision of subject information, the second, third, fourth and fifth data protection principles and certain of the subject rights created by the Act. Therefore, if the FSA makes a legitimate request for information, the Act does not operate so as to prevent the organisation from responding and disclosing personal information to the regulator.

As well as authorising the disclosure of personal information to the FSA, this exemption also covers the disclosure of personal information by the FSA as required by law. In this context the FSMA applies to restrict disclosures. In particular, any unauthorised disclosure of regulatory information is a criminal offence,[5] subject to certain exemptions. This means that the FSA must not disclose information relating to the business of any person that it has obtained for the purposes of its regulatory duty. If such information is legitimately disclosed to a third party under another statutory provision, this restriction also binds that third party from onward disclosure.

The restriction in the FSMA goes further than data protection law. First, it applies to information relating to corporate entities and partnerships, since it is not restricted to personal information and, second, it applies to business information relating to any person, and it is not restricted to regulated parties nor to living individuals.

There are some lawful disclosures of information relating to business activities obtained for the purposes of regulatory activity. These are:[6]

- with the consent of the person or organisation to whom the information relates;

- information that is already in public domain;

- information in summary form so that there is no relation to any particular person or organisation;

- the so-called 'Gateway exemptions';

- disclosure required for the purposes of a criminal investigation or criminal proceedings.

---

4   The Data Protection Act 1998, section 35.
5   Financial Services and Markets Act 2000, section 352.
6   Financial Services and Markets Act 2000 (Disclosure of Confidential Information) Regulations 2001, Statutory Instrument 2001/2188.

The 'Gateway exemptions' exist to assist the FSA and other regulatory bodies to carry out regulatory work, for example, to allow information to be checked with other regulatory authorities, including those in other legal jurisdictions. Where a regulatory authority is located in a jurisdiction outside of the EEA data protection law operates to restrict the transfer of personal information.[7] To make a transfer outside of the EEA, the FSA is restricted to those cases where it can show a necessity in order to perform an important public interest function, otherwise it must make the transfer only if it is satisfied that there is adequate protection for personal information transferred by carrying out an 'adequacy test', as explained in Chapter 11.

OTHER PROCESSING FOR REGULATORY PURPOSES

Processing personal information for purposes of regulatory activity benefits from another exemption in the Act. In this context, 'regulatory activity' means consumer protection activities in relation to banking, insurance, investment and other financial services, and corporate compliance. It also covers the regulation of charities, the activities of the Health and Safety Executive, Ombudsmen and the Office of Fair Trading.

The exemption[8] applies to exempt regulatory activity from subject information provisions, in any case where the application of those provisions would be likely to prejudice the proper discharge of the regulator's functions. The term 'subject information provisions' means the right of subject access and the obligation under the first principle to provide individuals to whom the personal information relates with information about the organisation and the purposes for which it processes their personal information. This exemption will be used, for example, where an on-going enquiry could be jeopardised if it were to be in the public domain and it allows the regulator to keep its investigations secret for as long as is necessary in order that it can carry out its obligations effectively.

THE FSA APPROACH TO DATA PROTECTION REGULATION OF MEMBER FIRMS

The FSA has adopted a risk-based approach[9] to regulation and the application of its resources to supervise and monitor regulated firms. Taking this approach, the main threat in terms of data protection compliance is likely to arise in relation to consumer business, although the FSA regulates significant non-consumer business, such as

---

7   The eighth data protection principle, see Chapter 11.
8   Set out in The Data Protection Act 1998, section 31.
9   Financial Services Authority (2003) *Risk-based Approach to Supervision of Banks*. Available from www.fsa.gov.uk.

reinsurance and Lloyds business, shipping for example, some banking and markets and exchanges generally.

Generally, the FSA does not investigate individual complaints about data protection breaches as such. Initially, complaints are referred back to the firm involved and, if the matter is not resolved, an individual might be advised to take the matter up with the Information Commissioner by way of requesting an assessment. However, the FSA reserves the right to investigate data protection breaches and will do so if it seems that a breach is a systemic problem either for one particular firm or across the industry.

RECRUITMENT OF APPROVED PERSONS

One of the key principles of FSA regulation is that financial services practitioners (approved persons, authorised persons and appointed representatives) should be fit and proper. Enforcement of the fit and proper principle requires that certain checks be carried out. The 'Fit and Proper Test for Approved Persons' includes checks on the individual's honesty, integrity and reputation. The list of matters that must be considered by the regulator and the employer[10] of individuals to carry out the role of approved person, authorised person or appointed representative, includes the following:

- criminal offences, with particular consideration being given to offences of dishonesty, fraud and financial crime;

- disciplinary hearings or investigations carried out by the FSA or any other regulatory authority or professional body;

- qualifications, training and experience to establish competence to carry out the controlled function;

- financial soundness.

This means that when recruiting, an organisation must make enquiries into the background of the prospective employee and their personal and professional conduct. It must also take into account the knowledge and skills of the individual in relation to the knowledge and skills required for the role and take reasonable steps to obtain sufficient and verifiable information about the individual's previous relevant activities and training. The information gathering part of the exercise depends upon obtaining personal information relating to the applicant from former employers and independent referees. The industry standard, based on the *FSA Handbook* is for 'full and frank disclosure', which runs counter to the current trend of limiting responses to

---

10 Under the FSMA, section 59, approval requires firms to take reasonable care to ensure that no person performs a controlled function without approval from the FSA.

reference requests to simple confirmation of the dates between which the individual was employed, if any response is forthcoming at all. 'Full and frank disclosure' is best made with the full knowledge and cooperation of the individual concerned in order that the subject information requirements are adequately addressed.

Several issues arise in this context. First, a reference includes personal information relating to the referee, their name, position and opinions, and the organisation may face a dilemma balancing the rights of the referee to privacy against the right of the employee to know what is in the reference. Second, there is the use of sensitive categories of data relating to criminal convictions, allegations of criminal offences and criminal proceedings.

INFORMATION RELATING TO THIRD PARTIES IN REFERENCES

When an employee exercises the right of access to information that the employer holds, the employer is in the unenviable position of having to decide whether, in all the circumstances, it is reasonable to override any promises of confidentiality made to referees in favour of full disclosure to the individual. The Act recognises that there are circumstances in which a data controller cannot comply with a subject access request without disclosing information that relates to, and identifies, another individual (a 'third party').[11] In such circumstances, the data controller must seek the consent of the third party to the disclosure and, failing to obtain such consent, it must decide whether or not it is reasonable in all the circumstances to comply with the request without the consent of the other individual. One of the legal points confirmed by the Court of Appeal in the Durant case,[12] is that the duty to protect personal information relating to a third party when responding to a subject access request is qualified. Data controllers are required to balance the rights of the enquirer against the rights of any third parties whose personal information comprises part of the information requested by the enquirer.

Many references are provided on a 'confidential' basis, in fact the term 'confidential reference' is frequently used to describe employment references. This promise of confidentiality may be challenged if the subject of the reference requests access to it. In many cases, an individual will easily be able to identify the referee from the reference, even where the name of the referee is withheld. The name of the referee and their opinions constitute personal information. Under the Act opinions are specifically included as personal information,[13] so an adverse opinion included in a reference is disclosable to the subject if an access request is received. Given the highly regulated environment and the potentially significant impact of an adverse reference, it is hard

---

11   The Data Protection Act 1998, section 7(4).

12   *Durant* v. *Financial Services Authority* [2003] EWCA Civ 1746].

13   The Data Protection Act 1998, section 1(1).

to envisage circumstances when a promise of confidentiality to a referee could be reasonably upheld if that party continues to decline to let the individual see the offending reference and the reference cannot be anonymised so that the identity of the third party is protected. What is certain is that whichever choice the prospective employer makes, disclosing or withholding the information, it is likely to upset one of the parties involved.

Outgoing references

When called upon to provide a reference, the organisation should have a clear policy that includes the names or titles of persons who are authorised to give references on its behalf. This policy should be communicated to all staff so that no one takes it upon themselves to provide a reference without due authority. The policy should also ensure that references are not dispatched unless the individual has requested that information be provided to future employers. This is an aspect that should be covered at exit interview, asking the leaver to confirm whether or not approaches for references should be dealt with.

The organisation's policy on granting access to outgoing references should be clear and communicated to all those who are authorised to give references. There is an exemption from subject access for references in the hands of the referee, although this is of little benefit once the reference has been issued, as the recipient of the reference has no similar exemption. However, the exemption will protect unsent references, drafts and such like.

The FSA takes the view that member firms are required to supply full references in relation to 'approved persons'. The FSA does not see that this will give rise to any problems so long as individuals are made aware of the disclosure regime.

USE OF SENSITIVE DATA

Some categories of information are defined as 'sensitive data' in the Act. They include information relating to criminal offences, criminal proceedings and alleged offences. Enquiries to satisfy the 'fit and proper' test for employees and agents may include obtaining such information. The FSA requires organisations to make enquiries into the background of prospective 'approved persons', 'authorised persons' and 'appointed representatives', including their honesty, integrity and reputation. In particular, when putting such persons forward for approval by the FSA, it will have regard to matters including criminal offences (the Rehabilitation of Offences Act 1974 is disapplied in these circumstances). Of particular concern are offences of dishonesty, fraud and financial crime, and adverse findings in civil proceedings relating to misconduct or fraud.

Organisations that process sensitive categories of information are required to authorise their processing activity by reference to one or more conditions for fair processing of sensitive data set out in one of the schedules to the Act. The conditions are considered in Chapter 4 on the first data protection principle. They allow processing in very restricted and prescribed circumstances. The commonly applicable conditions for fair processing of sensitive data in relation to employment vetting are:

- where processing is necessary to meet a legal obligation in connection with employment;

- with the explicit consent of the individual concerned.

Processing necessary to meet a legal obligation in connection with employment

Most legal obligations in connection with employment arise in relation to a legal duty owed to the employee. This could also apply in the circumstances of processing sensitive data to ensure that a prospective employee meets the 'fit and proper' criteria. The organisation is under a legal duty to comply with the FSA rules.

Explicit consent

The view of the Information Commissioner is that consent should be considered only when other options have been exhausted. However, it seems to be wholly appropriate grounds to justify processing information about an individual's criminal record in connection with a position of responsibility in their workplace. Individuals who choose to make a career in financial services are by now aware of the requirements for honesty and integrity and the 'fit and proper' test can hardly be news. Therefore, full disclosure of the intended investigation should be made and consent to the processing of any sensitive data arising from that investigation obtained.

Consent is defined in the EC Directive on Data Protection[14] as a freely given indication of approval. In relation to processing sensitive data, the requirement for 'explicit' consent indicating a high degree of disclosure to the individual about the sensitive data required and the processing activity to enable their consent to be informed and specific.

WHISTLE BLOWING

The regulatory regime encourages organisations to report their own breaches of legal obligation and regulatory rules ('notifiable events'). FSA rules also encourage

---

14 EC Directive 95/46/EC.

organisations to have internal whistle-blowing arrangements so that staff can report problems internally. Where the organisation is corrupt, individuals are encouraged to report such breaches externally. In this context, the group of individuals most likely to be aware of breaches of rules and attempts to cover them up are the employees. The Public Interest Disclosure Act 1998 (PIDA) was introduced to offer some protection to employees who make a qualifying disclosure. A qualifying disclosure may concern, for example, criminal offences, breaches of legal obligation, miscarriages of justice or health and safety risks.

Obviously, whistle blowing involves disclosing information about the organisation and it is likely to involve specific references to individuals. Where an individual blows the whistle on a criminal offence, for example, theft, obtaining money by deception or fraud, section 29 of the Data Protection Act provides certain exemptions, including an exemption from the first and second data protection principles. Therefore the disclosure of personal information intrinsic to the details of the crime is not in breach of the data protection principles even though the disclosure may not be consistent with the stated purposes for which personal information is being processed.

There is a difference where an individual blows the whistle on an activity that, although not a criminal offence, is a breach of regulatory rules. The disclosure of personal information by an individual to a regulator in this situation may in fact be an unauthorised disclosure. However, the Information Commissioner accepts that whistle blowing on a breach of the rules amounts to a legal obligation and is therefore exempt from data protection restrictions pursuant to section 35 of the Act which exempts disclosures required by law or made in connection with legal proceedings from the requirement to keep personal information confidential.

To complete the protection for individuals who blow the whistle on criminal activity or breaches of regulatory rules, PIDA provides that a qualifying disclosure does not breach any duty of confidentiality owed by the individual, including any confidentiality clauses in their contract of employment.

CHAPTER 24

Conflict between Laws and Regulation

In the UK, laws are based on Acts of Parliament (statutes) and court decisions in previous, similar cases that set precedents. When new statutes are introduced, they have to fit into an existing regulatory framework and it is possible that the objectives of one statute may frustrate or be frustrated by the objectives of another statute. Great care is taken when drafting legislation to minimise the impact of new statutes on existing law, but new legislation may still have to find a place in the legal pecking order.

The financial services industry is heavily regulated and various regulations, including those of the FSA, serve to add another layer of complexity when considering the interaction of legal authorities.

This chapter considers how data protection law fits in with other legislation and with financial regulation in particular. It is not intended to be an in-depth consideration of the subject of conflict of laws, which is a legal discipline in its own right. It is intended to help put the Data Protection Act 1998 (the Act) into context and to explain the circumstances when data protection law might not apply. For example, is security being breached when the police bring a warrant to search the premises? Is a disclosure being made when the regulator asks to look at specific client files that contain personal information? This chapter seeks to address the question of why some activities involving personal information are permitted when they appear to be contrary to data protection law.

The primary way to determine the precedence of laws is in the text of the relevant statutes. There are several provisions in the Act that are qualified by exemptions and exceptions 'as required by law' and other exemptions for regulatory activity.

DETERMINING PRECEDENCE – PROVISIONS IN THE DATA PROTECTION ACT 1998

PUBLISHING PERSONAL INFORMATION

Section 34 of the Act lists certain exemptions from key areas of data protection law if the organisation is under a statutory duty to make personal information available to the public in some way. Applying the first data protection principle, ordinarily it would be necessary to advise individuals at the time of obtaining personal information from them that it will be published. This fact is relevant to the decision of the individual to provide personal information as requested. However, where the organisation is fulfilling a statutory duty by publishing information, that statutory obligation will take precedence over the duty of confidentiality otherwise owed to individuals.

This is probably most important in situations where a new statutory duty arises and the organisation is bound by subject information given previously and therefore lacks the authority to process the personal information by publishing it. Consider the obligations to publish personal information relating to directors and officers of the company under company law and corporate governance. These obligations have been transformed in recent years so that a lot of personal information must now be published. Existing contracts with directors probably would not have envisaged some of the more recent disclosure requirements. Nevertheless, the duty to publish information including personal information overrides data protection considerations as a result of section 34 of the Act.

DISCLOSURE OF PERSONAL INFORMATION

Another potential conflict of legal requirements is where a statute requires information to be disclosed, perhaps not publicly, but certainly outside the organisation and its advisers. Section 35 of the Act provides an exemption where, for example, disclosure of financial information relating to staff is required by the Inland Revenue, the Child Benefit Agency or HM Revenue & Customs. Section 35 likewise authorises the disclosure of personal information in connection with money laundering prevention measures.

Section 35 also applies to authorise disclosures of personal information required by a Court or any rule of law. This exemption allows organisations to comply with warrants and Court Orders, for example, to hand over client files or employee files to the authorities, which would otherwise be in breach of duties of confidentiality and non-disclosure under data protection law.

Where disclosure is necessary for the purpose of obtaining legal advice, exercising or defending legal rights, or in connection with any legal proceedings, the non-disclosure provisions are waived under section 35(2). This would apply, for example, if an employer sought legal advice in connection with an employment issue.

Where a criminal offence is suspected, section 29 of the Act authorises disclosure of personal information and also has effect to authorise disclosure with the aim of preventing a crime, and the apprehension or prosecution of offenders. This is a key exemption when making relevant reports for purposes of money laundering prevention or where an individual or group of individuals blows the whistle on criminal and alleged criminal activities.

KEEPING REGULATORY ACTIVITY CONFIDENTIAL

Processing personal information for purposes of regulatory activity benefits from another exemption set out in section 31 of the Act. In this context, 'regulatory activity' means consumer protection activities in relation to banking, insurance, investment and other financial services and corporate compliance. It also covers the regulation of charities, the activities of the Health and Safety Executive, Ombudsmen and the Office of Fair Trading. The exemption applies to exempt regulatory activity from subject information provisions, that is, the duty to provide individuals to whom the personal information refers with information about the organisation and the purposes for which it processes their personal information. Subject information also includes the right of subject access.

GUIDANCE FROM THE INFORMATION COMMISSIONER

In *Legal Guidance* published in December 2001, the Information Commissioner recommended a two-part test to determine whether or not an organisation can rely on an exemption. First, it must determine which exemption it seeks to rely on:

- section 29: the crime and taxation exemption;

- section 34: the exemption to allow publication of personal information required by statute;

- section 35: the disclosure of personal information required by law.

Second, the organisation must consider the specific exemption it requires. The exemptions apply to exempt organisations from a number of the data protection principles, in particular, the requirement to provide subject information pursuant to the first principle and some of the subject rights created under the Act. The organisation is entitled to disapply these provisions only to the extent that they inhibit the performance of a legal obligation. These exemptions do not operate to provide a blanket authority to override the provisions of the Act.

In particular, the Information Commissioner says:[1]

> *if the data controller is well aware when he collects the data that at some point he is likely to have to make disclosure of those data under statute, it would not be incompatible with the disclosure to notify data subjects at*

---

1   *Legal Guidance*, para. 5.9.

the time the data are collected from them, that such disclosure is likely.
The First Principle should not be disapplied generally.

PROVISIONS IN OTHER LEGISLATION

The Freedom of Information Act 2000 (FOI) is designed to work alongside data protection law to encourage the open flow of information from public bodies. However, it should not compromise privacy for individuals. Section 40 of the FOI provides for information comprising personal data within the meaning of the Act to be withheld from access requests made under FOI subject to certain exceptions in relation to individuals who act in an official capacity and who take decisions of public importance.

CONFLICTS

When the text of a statute does not specifically provide for it to take precedence over, or be subject to, the Act and the exemptions in the Act itself do not make the position any clearer, the final resort is to the Courts.

CONCLUSION

The view of the Information Commissioner is that organisations should seek to comply with data protection law rather than seeking exemptions from it. However, there are circumstances where the exemptions are a necessary mechanism to allow organisations and regulators to carry out their legal obligations. Within the framework of the Act are provisions for exempting organisations from the duty to maintain confidentiality of personal information where that duty conflicts with a public duty to disclose information in specific circumstances. The regulator will apply the exemptions narrowly; organisations are encouraged to consider carefully the extent to which an exemption can be reasonably applied.

Bibliography

Association of British Insurers (1999) *Genetic Testing – ABI Code of Practice*. Available from www.abi.org.uk.

Advertising Standards Authority (2003) *British Code of Advertising, Sales Promotion and Direct Marketing* (11th edition). London: ASA.

Banking Code Standards Board (2005) *The Banking Code*. London: British Bankers' Association.

Direct Marketing Association (2004) *Best Practice Guidelines – Data in Direct Marketing*. Available from www.dma.org.uk.

Direct Marketing Association (2004) *DM Code of Practice* (3rd edition). London: Direct Marketing Association.

Direct Marketing Association (2004) *Email Marketing Council, Best Practice Guidelines*. Available from www.dma.org.uk.

Financial Services Authority (2003) *Reducing Money Laundering Risk – Know Your Customer and Anti-Money Laundering Monitoring* (DP22). Available from www.fsa.gov.uk.

Financial Services Authority (2003) *Risk-based Approach to Supervising Banks*. Available from www.fsa.gov.uk.

Financial Services Authority (2004) *The Protection of Regulatory Information under English Law*. Available from www.fsa.gov.uk.

Financial Services Authority (2005) *Offshore Operations: Industry Feedback*. Available from www.fsa.gov.uk/pubs/other/offshore_ops.pdf.

Financial Services Authority (2005) *The FSA Handbook*. Available from www.fsahandbook.info/FSA.

Information Commissioner (1994) *The Data Protection Principles*. London: Data Protection Registrar.

Information Commissioner (1994) *The Data Protection Principles: Third Series*. London: Data Protection Registrar.

Information Commissioner (1994) *The Guidelines: Third Series*. London: Data Protection Registrar.

Information Commissioner (1999) *The Eighth Data Protection Principle and Transborder Dataflows*. London: Data Protection Registrar.

Information Commissioner (2000) *CCTV Code of Practice*. London: Data Protection Registrar.

Information Commissioner (2000) *International Transfers of Personal Data*. London: Data Protection Registrar.

Information Commissioner (2000) *Subject Access Rights and Third Party Information.* London: Data Protection Registrar.

Information Commissioner (2001) *Annual Report Summary for 2001.* Available from www.informationcommissioner.gov.uk.

Information Commissioner (2001) *Guide to Data Protection Auditing.* London: Data Protection Registrar.

Information Commissioner (2001) *The Data Protection Act 1998: Legal Guidance.* London: Data Protection Registrar.

Information Commissioner (2002) *The Plumstones* (educational CD-ROM). London: Data Protection Registrar.

Information Commissioner (2003) *Annual Report and Accounts.* Available from www.informationcommissioner.gov.uk.

Information Commissioner (2004) *Corporate Registration on TPS.* London: Data Protection Registrar.

Information Commissioner (2004) *Electronic Communications Guidance.* London: Data Protection Registrar.

Information Commissioner (2004) *How to Manage your Personal Data under the Data Protection Act* (comicbook-style guide). London: Data Protection Registrar.

Information Commissioner (2005) *The Employment Practices Data Protection Code.* Available from www.informationcommissioner.gov.uk.

Press Complaints Commission (2005) *Data Protection Act, Journalism and the PCC Code.* Available from www.pcc.org.uk.

University of Sheffield (2004) *What Are 'Personal Data'?* (Study carried out on behalf of the Information Commissioner.) Available from www.informationcommissioner.gov.uk.

Index

(Law cases are indexed under 'cases')